This book belongs to:

LEISURE ARTS, INC.
Little Rock, Arkansas

down Santa Claus Lane

EDITORIAL STAFF

Editor-in-Chief: Anne Van Wagner Childs. *Executive Director:* Sandra Graham Case. *Executive Editor:* Susan Frantz Wiles. *Publications Director:* Carla Bentley. *Creative Art Director:* Gloria Bearden. *Production Art Director:* Melinda Stout. PRODUCTION — *Managing Editor:* Susan White Sullivan. *Senior Editor:* Carla A. Jones. *Project Coordinators:* Stephanie Gail Sharp and Andrea Ahlen. DESIGN — *Design Director:* Patricia Wallenfang Sowers. *Designer:* Linda Diehl Tiano. EDITORIAL — *Associate Editor:* Linda L. Trimble. *Editorial Writers:* Tammi Williamson Bradley and Terri Leming Davidson. *Copy Editor:* Laura Lee Weland. ART — *Book/Magazine Art Director:* Diane M. Ghegan. *Senior Production Artist:* Stephen L. Mooningham. *Production Artist:* Mark A. Hawkins. *Art Assistants:* Hubrith E. Esters, Deborah Taylor, and M. Katherine Yancey. *Photography Stylist:* Christina Tiano. *Typesetters:* Cindy Lumpkin, Stephanie Cordero, and Larry Flaxman. ADVERTISING AND DIRECT MAIL — *Copywriters:* Steven M. Cooper, Marla Shivers, and Tena Kelley Vaughn. *Designer:* Rhonda H. Hestir. *Art Director:* Jeff Curtis. *Artists:* Linda Lovette Smart and Angie Griffin.

BUSINESS STAFF

Publisher: Steve Patterson. *Controller:* Tom Siebenmorgen. *Retail Sales Director:* Richard Tignor. *Retail Marketing Director:* Pam Stebbins. *Retail Customer Services Director:* Margaret Sweetin. *Marketing Manager:* Russ Barnett. *Executive Director of Marketing and Circulation:* Guy A. Crossley. *Fulfillment Manager:* Byron L. Taylor. *Print Production Manager:* Laura Lockhart. *Print Production Coordinator:* Nancy Reddick Lister.

CREDITS

PHOTOGRAPHY: Ken West, Larry Pennington, and Karen Busick Shirey of Peerless Photography, Little Rock, Arkansas; and Jerry R. Davis of Jerry Davis Photography, Little Rock, Arkansas. COLOR SEPARATIONS: Magna IV Color Imaging of Little Rock, Arkansas. CUSTOM FRAMING: Nelda and Carlton Newby of Creative Framers, North Little Rock, Arkansas. PHOTO LOCATIONS: The homes of Martha Bradshaw, Sandra Cook, Janet Feurig, Shirley Held, Linda Wardlaw, and Susan Wildung.

Library of Congress Catalog Number 94-75391
International Standard Book Number 0-942237-37-4

INTRODUCTION

For many of us, Santa Claus has been a part of our holiday celebrations since earliest childhood. In younger years, we delighted in the surprises he left beneath the tree; as adults, his spirit of love and sharing reminds us of the true meaning of Christmas. A blending of secular and religious images, the familiar red-clad figure we know today is quite different from the gift-bringers of years past. Turn-of-the-century artists found a special joy in re-creating these many faces of Santa in beautifully detailed drawings and paintings. In Santa Remembered, the first book in this series, we brought you a stunning collection of portraits adapted from this Victorian-Era artwork. In this nostalgic volume, we continue that tradition with timeless images of Santa captured in heirloom-quality designs. Along with lovely framed portraits, you'll find the kindly gift-giver depicted on stockings, ornaments, and even clothing. So turn the page, and join us for a magical journey Down Santa Claus Lane!

TABLE OF CONTENTS

Chart on pages 50-51

6

SANTA IN TOYLAND

Santa's North Pole workshop is busy all year long, but on Christmas Eve it becomes a hive of activity as the jolly old elf works to fill last-minute requests from hopeful children. As little ones drift off to sleep on that momentous night, their dreams are sweetened by visions of Santa's magical toyland and the wonderful treats they'll discover tucked inside their Christmas stockings.

Charts on pages 55-57

8

TIMELESS IMAGES

The appearance of Santa has changed over the years, but always he is depicted as gentle, kind, benevolent, and merry — the timeless attributes we cherish. Reflecting several different images of the beloved gift-bringer, these miniature portraits will bring the elegance of yesteryear to your tree.

9

UP ON THE HOUSETOP

Up on the housetop reindeer pause,
Out jumps good old Santa Claus;
Down through the chimney with lots of toys,
All for the little ones, Christmas joys.

— *TRADITIONAL*

Chart on pages 58-59

11

Charts on pages 60 and 62

all through the house

We all love dressing our homes in Christmas finery. Along with the traditional tree, smaller accents and decorations spread cheer all through the house. These beautifully stitched pillows lend a festive air to a sofa or chair.

Chart on page 78

Charts on pages 61 and 92

*T*he holly's up, the house is all bright,
The tree is ready, the candles alight;
Rejoice and be glad, all children tonight.

— *FROM AN OLD CAROL*

Chart on page 63

ST. NICK AFGHAN

Immortalized for all time in the classic holiday poem "The Night Before Christmas," old St. Nick is loved by children the world over. To bring added warmth to Christmas Eve, a richly colored afghan is adorned with the kindly visage of this eagerly awaited visitor.

The stump of a pipe he held tight in his teeth,
And the smoke it encircled his head like a wreath.

— CLEMENT CLARKE MOORE

Chart on pages 64-65

THE CHILDREN'S FRIEND

Jolly old Saint Nicholas
Lean your ear this way;
Don't you tell a single soul
What I'm going to say:
Christmas Eve is coming soon;
Now you dear old man,
Whisper what you'll bring to me,
Tell me if you can.

— *TRADITIONAL*

Chart on pages 66-67

ENTER

With
A Happy Heart

Chart on pages 68-69

A CHRISTMAS WELCOME

The holiday season is a special time to open our homes to family and friends through joyous parties and informal gatherings. The kindly gentleman on this welcoming banner greets visitors at the door, bidding them to "Enter with a happy heart."

BABY'S FIRST CHRISTMAS

The celebration of a baby's very first Christmas brings an added measure of joy and wonder to the holidays. In this touching scene, Santa steals a moment from his busy schedule to gaze wistfully at the family's newest arrival.

Chart on pages 70-71

23

MEMORY ALBUM

Recalling the joys of past Christmases is a special part of the holidays. As we create new memories, we also take time to pull out the family album and relive cherished moments from previous celebrations. This handsome photograph album, adorned with a nostalgic portrait of Santa, is the perfect place to store such precious memories.

Chart on page 72

AN ALL-AMERICAN CELEBRATION

Framed by the stars and stripes, Santa soars
o'er the land of the free on his yearly quest.
Images like this one may seem unusual to us
today, but turn-of-the-century artists often
mingled patriotism with holiday spirit.

Chart on pages 74-75

Charts on pages 76-77

28

Many American patriots displayed their love of country by trimming their Christmas trees with proudly waving flags and other star-spangled decorations. Reminding us of our proud national heritage, these all-American Santa ornaments will add a spirited touch to your holiday tree. A richly hued afghan shows the jolly old elf sporting a tricorn hat as he flies through the midnight sky.

Chart on pages 74-75

HANDSOME TREE SKIRT

With his rosy cheeks and flowing white beard, this hooded gentleman is typical of the Victorian image of St. Nicholas. A sprig of holly, symbolizing the blood of Christ and His gift of life "ever green," adds special meaning to the portrait. The handsome tree skirt is made from classic tartan plaid fabric, a popular pattern of the late 1800's.

Chart on page 78

HUMBLE VISITOR

Seeking refuge from the blustery winter night, this Christmas visitor peeks around the door to catch a glimpse of a candle-lit tree. His simple homespun robe and hooded cape reflect many early European images of the humble gift-bringer.

Chart on pages 80-81

LIGHTING THE WAY

When darkness falls on Christmas Eve, Santa sometimes needs a lamp to light his path. In this scene, the holiday visitor makes his way from house to house bearing a bag of toys for good children — and a bundle of switches for the naughty ones.

Chart on pages 82-83

35

childhood
TREASURES

*Every Christmas Eve, Santa delights children
the world over by filling their stockings with toys
and goodies. And whether it's a teddy bear for a
little boy or a dainty dolly for a little girl, he
always knows just what gift will please each
child. These personalized stockings and
coordinating ornaments are destined to become
treasured keepsakes of childhood.*

Chart on page 53

Chart on page 52

Chart on page 53

Chart on page 52

Chart on pages 84-85

CHRISTMAS TRAVELER

*During his yearly journey, Santa is occasionally spotted by
a few lucky children. Here, two ecstatic youngsters stop their
play to greet the Christmas traveler as he passes by.*

JOY TO THE WORLD

In years past, the Christkindl, or Christ Child,
was believed to bring the Christmas gifts in some
European countries. His radiant figure was as familiar
to children of the day as that of the good St. Nicholas.
This touching portrait of the kindly gentleman and
the Holy Infant reminds us of the great joy
that was born in Bethlehem.

Chart on pages 86-87

OLDE WORLD SANTAS

Today we usually envision the Christmas visitor
in a coat of bright red, but in years past he was often
seen clad in blue, green, or even brown. Featuring a
nostalgic collection of Olde World Santas, these lace-
trimmed bookmarks make unique tree decorations
or thoughtful remembrances for friends.

Charts on pages 88-89

holiday dressing

We all love the fun of dressing up in holiday style,
especially when our apparel features images of the jolly
old elf himself. This endearing vision of Santa feeding
a special treat to his reindeer adds Christmas charm to
a plain sweatshirt. The shiny jingle bells will sing
out a merry melody with every step you take.

Chart on page 91

Charts on pages 88 and 92

Chart on page 93

48

E mbellished clothing and accessories make wonderful gifts for friends — or for yourself! Portraits of old St. Nick transform ordinary sweaters into unique holiday wear, and the necklace and button covers will add a festive touch to any outfit.

Charts on pages 90 and 92

SANTA IN TOYLAND

Santa in Toyland Stocking (shown on page 6): The design was stitched over 2 fabric threads on an 18" x 24" piece of Mushroom Lugana (25 ct) with top of design 8" from one short edge of fabric. Three strands of floss were used for Cross Stitch and 1 strand for Backstitch and French Knots.

For stocking, you will need an 18" x 24" piece of Mushroom Lugana for backing, two 18" x 24" pieces of fabric for lining, 16½" x 10" piece of coordinating fabric for cuff, 2" x 5" piece of fabric for hanger, tracing paper, and fabric marking pencil.

Matching arrows of Stocking Pattern (page 96) to form one pattern, trace pattern onto tracing paper and add ½" seam allowance to all sides; cut out pattern. Referring to photo for placement, position pattern on wrong side of stitched piece; pin pattern in place. Use fabric marking pencil to draw around pattern; remove pattern and cut out on drawn line. Use pattern and cut **one** from backing fabric and **two** from lining fabric.

Matching right sides and leaving top edge open, use a ½" seam allowance to sew stitched piece and backing fabric together; clip seam allowance at curves and turn stocking right side out.

Matching right sides and leaving top edge open, use a ⅝" seam allowance to sew lining fabric together; trim seam allowance close to stitching. **Do not turn lining right side out.** With wrong sides facing, place lining inside stocking; baste lining and stocking together close to top edge.

Matching right sides and short edges of coordinating cuff fabric, use a ½" seam allowance to sew short edges together. Matching wrong sides and raw edges, fold cuff in half and press. Matching raw edges, place cuff inside stocking with cuff seam at center back of stocking. Use ½" seam allowance to sew cuff, stocking, and lining together. Fold cuff 4" over stocking and press.

For hanger, press each long edge of fabric strip ½" to center. Fold strip in half, matching long edges; sew close to folded edges. Matching short edges, fold hanger in half and blind stitch to inside of stocking at left seam.

Needlework adaptation by Nancy Dockter.

STITCH COUNT (126w x 150h)		
14 count	9"	x 10¾"
16 count	7⅞"	x 9⅜"
18 count	7"	x 8⅜"
22 count	5¾"	x 6⅞"

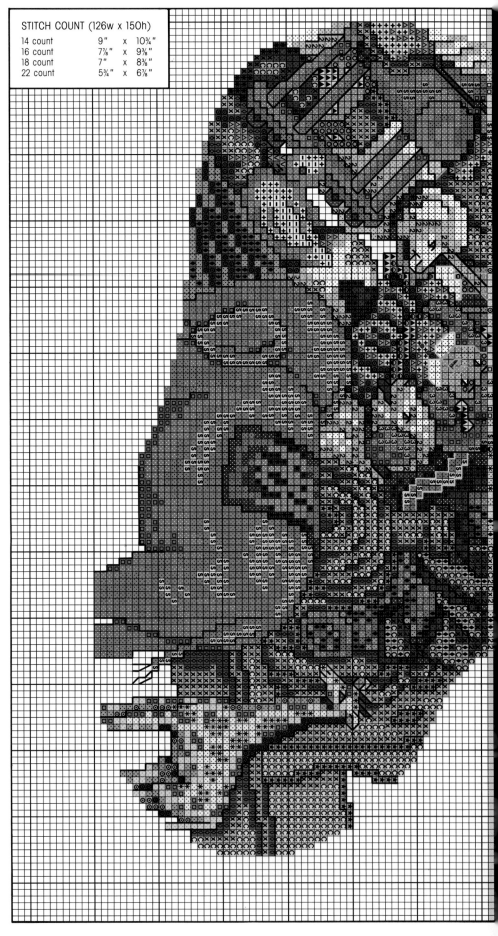

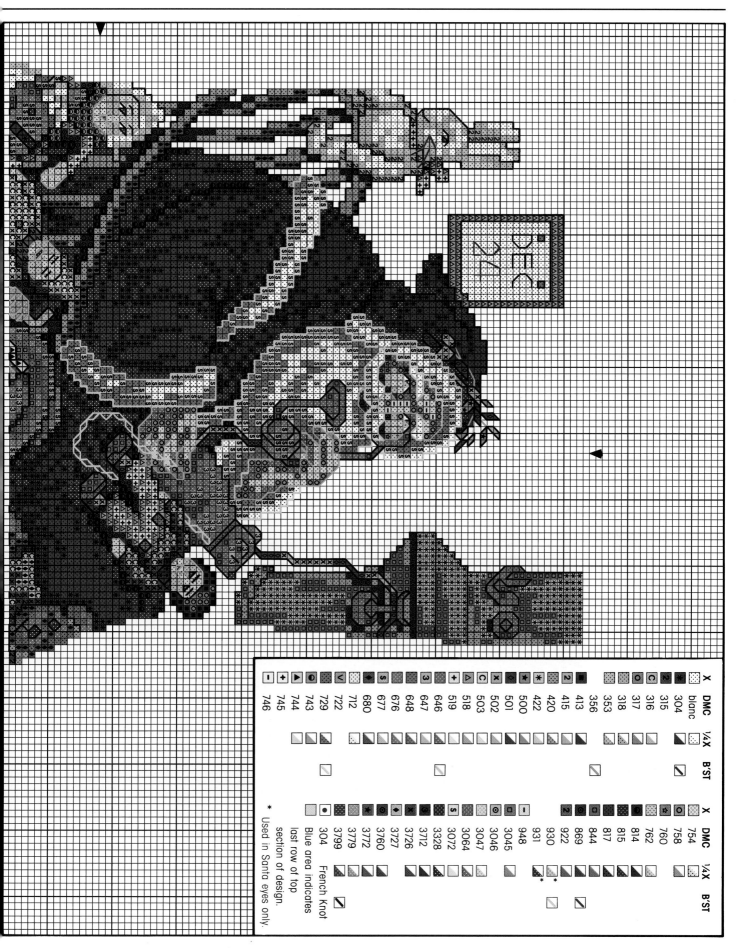

childhood treasures

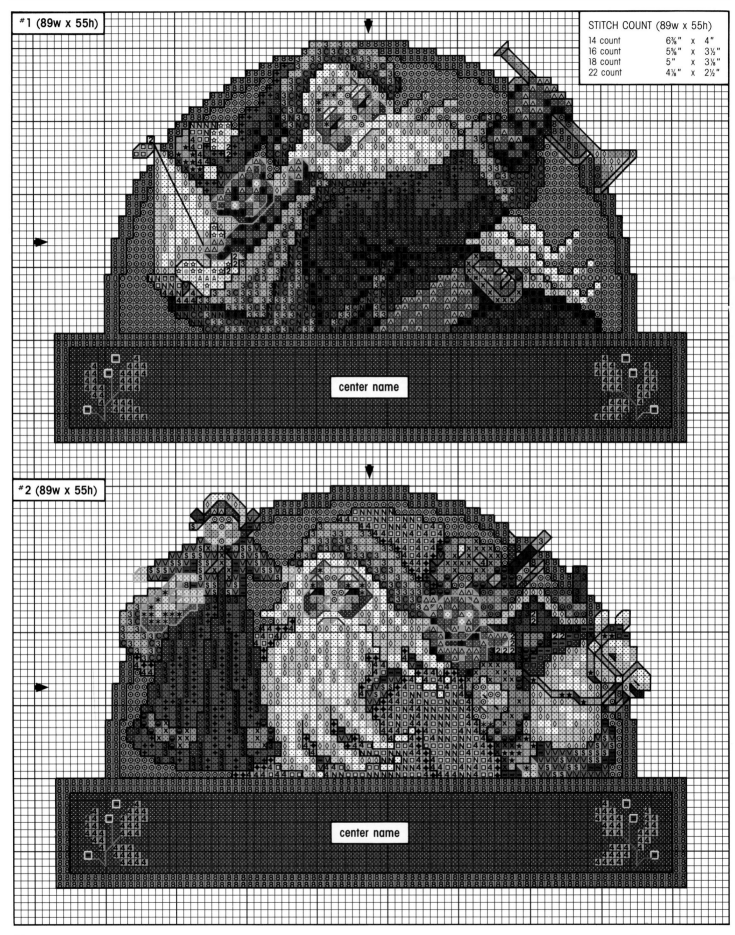

#1 (89w x 55h)

STITCH COUNT (89w x 55h)

14 count	6⅜"	x 4"
16 count	5⅝"	x 3½"
18 count	5"	x 3⅛"
22 count	4⅛"	x 2½"

center name

#2 (89w x 55h)

center name

X	DMC	¼X	½X	B'ST
	blanc			
	310			∕
X	312	∕		
	317			
	318	∕		
	321	∕		∕
	347	∕		
	349	∕		
	353		∕	
	356			∕
□	413	∕		
⊙	414	∕	▲	
	415			
△	420	∕		∕
	422	∕		
3	498	∕		
N	611			∕
—	666			∕
X	676	∕		
⊙	680	∕		
V	721	∕		
2	725	∕		
	726			
☆	727			
*	729	∕		
*	758	∕		
	760	∕		
◇	762			
⊙	806	∕		
■	814	∕		
	815	∕		
★	825			
	826	∕		
8	833	∕		
■	839	∕		
V	840	∕		
S	841	∕		
	869	∕		
◆	904			
4	905	∕		
□	906	∕		
N	907			
⊙ *	948 &	∕		
	754			
	3021	∕		
C	3032	∕		
	3033	∕		
	3064	∕		
	3328	∕		∕
	3779	∕		
	3781	∕		
3	3782	∕		
■	3799	∕		∕
⊙	310	French Knot		
●	321	French Knot		

* Use 2 strands of first floss color listed and 1 strand of second floss color listed.

Gifts for Girls and Boys Stockings (shown on pages 37 and 39): Designs #1 and #2 were each stitched over 2 fabric threads on a 17" x 12" piece of White Irish Linen (28 ct). Three strands of floss were used for Cross Stitch and 1 strand for Backstitch and French Knots. Personalize using the alphabet below; fill in background using DMC 3799 floss. (See Stocking Finishing, page 54.)

Needlework adaptation by Nancy Dockter.

Favorite Toy Ornaments (shown on pages 36 and 38): Designs #3 and #4 were each stitched over 2 fabric threads on a 9" square of White Irish Linen (28 ct). Three strands of floss were used for Cross Stitch and 1 strand for Half Cross Stitch, Backstitch, and French Knots. (See Ornament Finishing, page 54.)

Designed by Nancy Dockter.

#3 (27w x 34h)

#4 (36w x 30h)

childhood treasures

STOCKING FINISHING

(Shown on pages 37 and 39, charts on page 52.)

For each stocking, you will need a 15" x 6" piece of White Irish Linen for cuff backing, two 13" x 20" pieces of fabric for stocking, two 13" x 20" pieces of fabric for lining, 2" x 42" bias fabric strip and 42" length of ¼" dia. purchased cord for cording on stocking, 2" x 17" bias fabric strip and 17" length of ¼" dia. purchased cord for cording on cuff, 2" x 5" piece of fabric for hanger, tracing paper, and fabric marking pencil.

Centering design, trim stitched piece to measure 15" x 6".

For stocking pattern, match arrows of Stocking Pattern to form one pattern and trace pattern onto tracing paper; add a ½" seam allowance on all sides and cut out pattern. Matching right sides and raw edges, place stocking fabric pieces together; place pattern on fabric pieces and pin pattern in place. Use fabric marking pencil to draw around pattern; remove pattern and cut out on drawn line. Repeat with lining fabric pieces.

For stocking cording, center cord on wrong side of bias strip; matching long edges, fold strip over cord. Use a zipper foot to baste along length of strip close to cord; trim seam allowance to ½". Referring to photo for placement, match raw edges and baste cording to right side of one stocking piece. Trim away excess cording.

Matching right sides and leaving top open, use a ½" seam allowance to sew stocking pieces together. Clip seam allowance at curves and turn stocking right side out.

Matching right sides and leaving top edge open, use a ⅝" seam allowance to sew

lining pieces together; trim seam allowance close to stitching. **Do not turn lining right side out**. With wrong sides facing, place lining inside stocking. Baste stocking and lining together close to raw edges.

For stocking cuff, match right sides and short edges; fold stitched piece in half. Using a ½" seam allowance, sew short edges together. Repeat for cuff backing.

For cuff cording, center cord on wrong side of bias strip; matching long edges, fold strip over cord. Baste along length of strip close to cord; trim seam allowance to ½". Matching raw edges and beginning at seam, pin cording to right side of stitched piece at lower edge. Ends of cording should overlap approximately 2"; pin overlapping end out of the way. Starting 2" from beginning end of cording and ending 4" from overlapping end, baste cording to stitched piece. On overlapping end of cording, remove 2½" of basting; fold end of fabric back and trim cord so that it meets beginning end of cord. Fold end of fabric under ½"; wrap fabric over beginning end of cording. Finish basting cording to stitched piece.

Matching right sides, raw edges, and seams, use a ½" seam allowance to sew cuff and cuff backing together along lower edge of cuff; turn right side out and press. Baste cuff and cuff backing together close to raw edges.

Referring to photo and matching raw edges, place right side of cuff to inside of stocking with cuff back seam at center back of stocking. Use a ½" seam allowance to sew cuff and stocking together. Fold cuff 4¾" to outside of stocking and press.

For hanger, press each long edge of fabric strip ½" to center. Matching long edges, fold strip in half and sew close to folded edges. Fold hanger in half, matching short edges; refer to photo and blind stitch to inside of stocking.

ORNAMENT FINISHING

(Shown on pages 36 and 38, charts on page 53.)

For each ornament, you will need a 5½" dia. circle of White Irish Linen for backing, two 3½" dia. circles of adhesive mounting board, two 3½" dia. circles of batting, 2" x 15" bias fabric strip for cording, 15" length of ¼" dia. purchased cord, 6" length of ¼"w ribbon for hanger, and clear-drying craft glue.

Centering design, trim stitched piece to a 5½" dia. circle.

Remove paper from one piece of mounting board and press one batting piece onto mounting board. Repeat with remaining mounting board and batting.

Clip ½" into edge of stitched piece at ½" intervals. Center stitched piece over batting on one mounting board piece; fold edges of stitched piece to back of mounting board and glue in place. Repeat with backing fabric and remaining mounting board for ornament back.

For cording, center cord on wrong side of bias strip; matching long edges, fold strip over cord. Use a zipper foot to sew along length of strip close to cord; trim seam allowance to ½". Starting 2" from beginning of cording and at bottom center of stitched piece, glue cording seam allowance to wrong side of ornament front; stop 3" from overlapping end of cording. On overlapping end of cording, remove 2½" of basting; fold end of fabric back and trim cord so that it meets beginning end of cord. Fold end of fabric under ½"; wrap fabric over beginning end of cording. Finish gluing cording to stitched piece.

For hanger, fold ribbon in half, matching short edges; refer to photo and glue to wrong side of ornament front. Matching wrong sides, glue ornament front and back together.

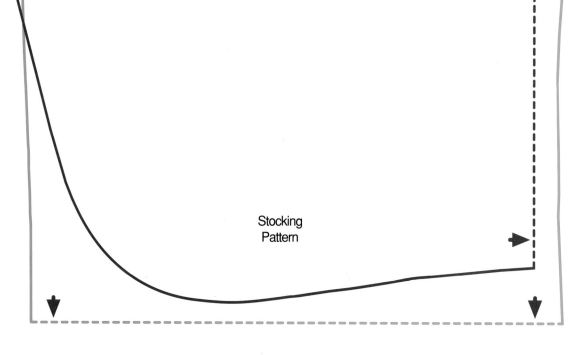

Stocking
Pattern

TIMELESS IMAGES

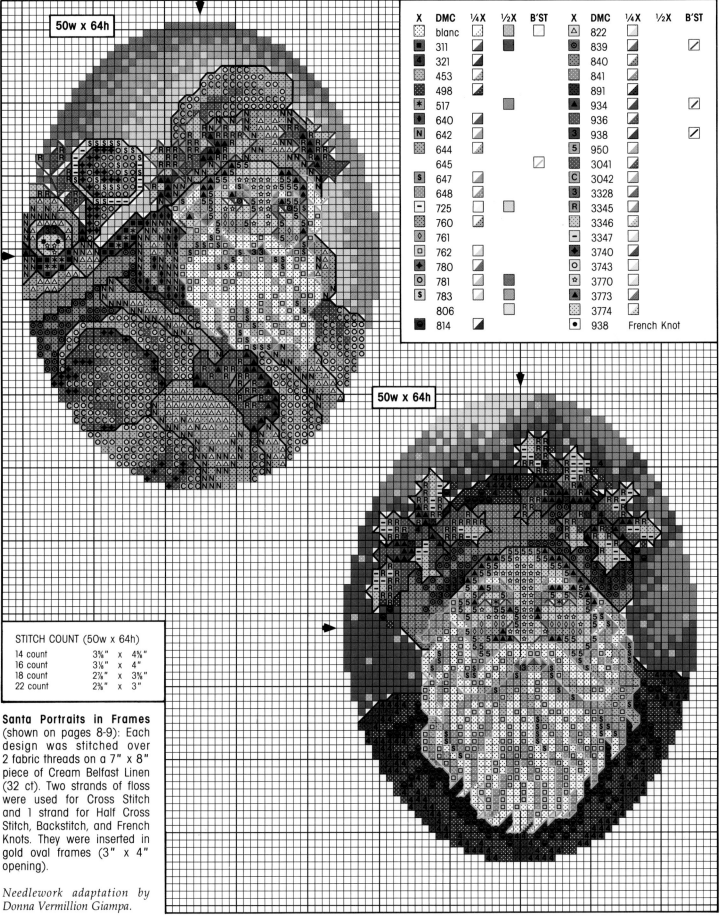

50w x 64h

50w x 64h

X	DMC	¼X	½X	B'ST		X	DMC	¼X	½X	B'ST
	blanc					△	822			
■	311					⊙	839			/
4	321						840			
	453						841			
	498					■	891			
*	517					▲	934			/
♦	640						936			
N	642					3	938			/
	644					5	950			
	645			/			3041			
S	647					C	3042			
	648					3	3328			
-	725					R	3345			
	760						3346			
◊	761					-	3347			
□	762					♦	3740			
♦	780					O	3743			
O	781					☆	3770			
S	783					▲	3773			
	806						3774			
◙	814					●	938	French Knot		

STITCH COUNT (50w x 64h)

14 count	3⅝"	x	4⅝"
16 count	3⅛"	x	4"
18 count	2⅞"	x	3½"
22 count	2⅜"	x	3"

Santa Portraits in Frames (shown on pages 8-9): Each design was stitched over 2 fabric threads on a 7" x 8" piece of Cream Belfast Linen (32 ct). Two strands of floss were used for Cross Stitch and 1 strand for Half Cross Stitch, Backstitch, and French Knots. They were inserted in gold oval frames (3" x 4" opening).

Needlework adaptation by Donna Vermillion Giampa.

TIMELESS IMAGES

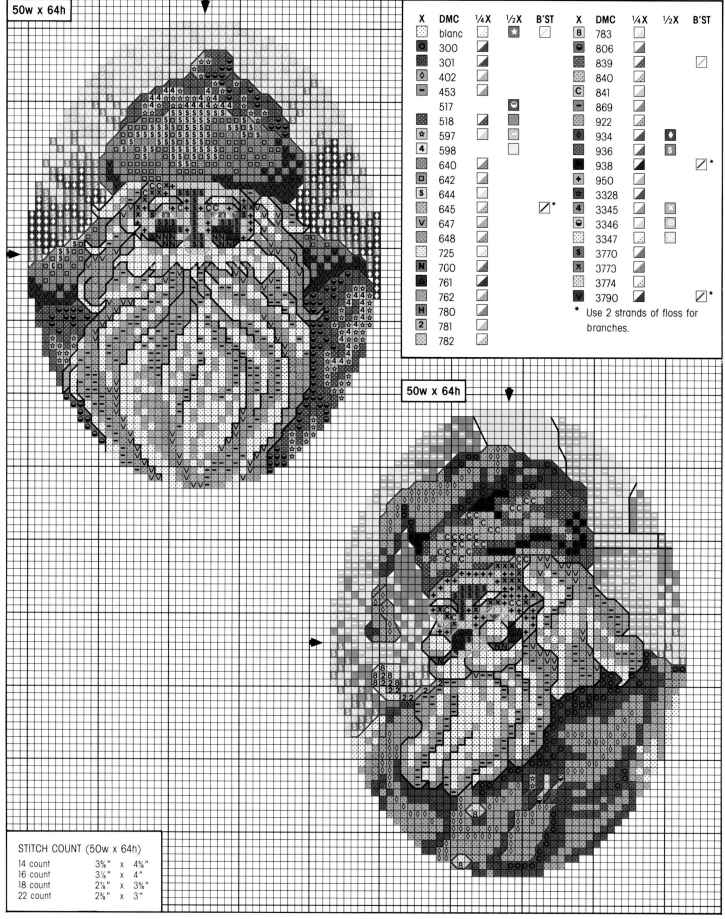

50w x 64h

X	DMC	¼X	½X	B'ST		X	DMC	¼X	½X	B'ST
	blanc		★			8	783			
◐	300					◉	806			
	301						839			
◇	402						840			
−	453					C	841			
	517		◓			−	869			
	518						922			
☆	597		−			◇	934		◆	
4	598						936		S	
	640						938			*
	642					+	950			
S	644					☆	3328			
	645			*		4	3345		X	
V	647					◓	3346		◉	
	648						3347			
	725					S	3770			
N	700					X	3773			
◣	761						3774			
	762					V	3790			*
H	780									
2	781									
	782									

* Use 2 strands of floss for branches.

50w x 64h

STITCH COUNT (50w x 64h)

14 count	3⅝"	x	4⅝"
16 count	3⅛"	x	4"
18 count	2⅞"	x	3⅝"
22 count	2⅜"	x	3"

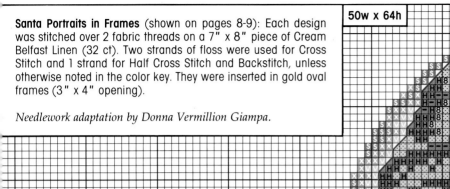

Santa Portraits in Frames (shown on pages 8-9): Each design was stitched over 2 fabric threads on a 7" x 8" piece of Cream Belfast Linen (32 ct). Two strands of floss were used for Cross Stitch and 1 strand for Half Cross Stitch and Backstitch, unless otherwise noted in the color key. They were inserted in gold oval frames (3" x 4" opening).

Needlework adaptation by Donna Vermillion Giampa.

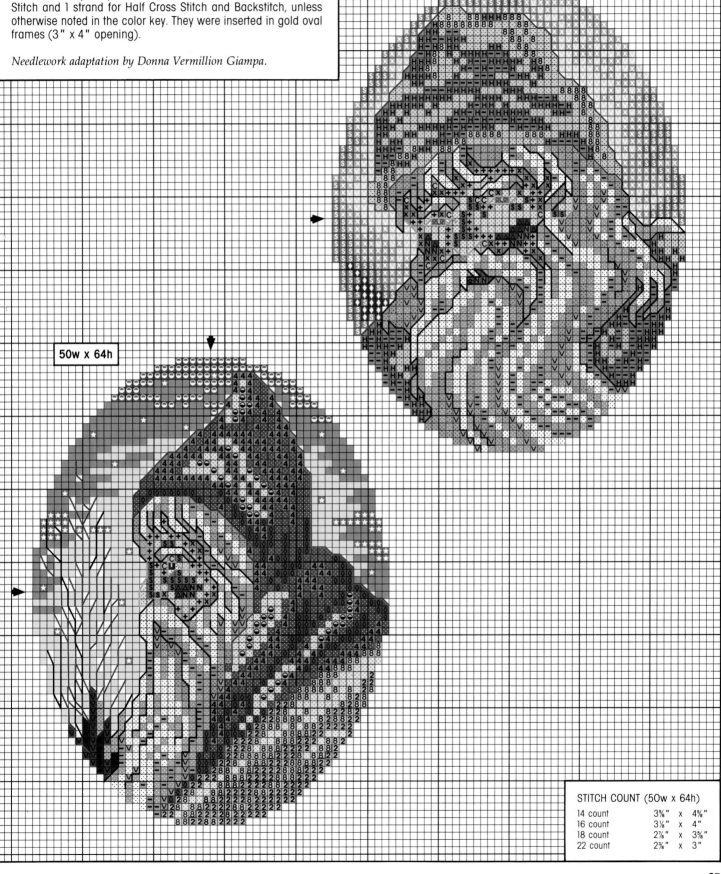

50w x 64h

50w x 64h

STITCH COUNT (50w x 64h)		
14 count	3⅝"	x 4⅝"
16 count	3⅛"	x 4"
18 count	2⅞"	x 3⅝"
22 count	2⅜"	x 3"

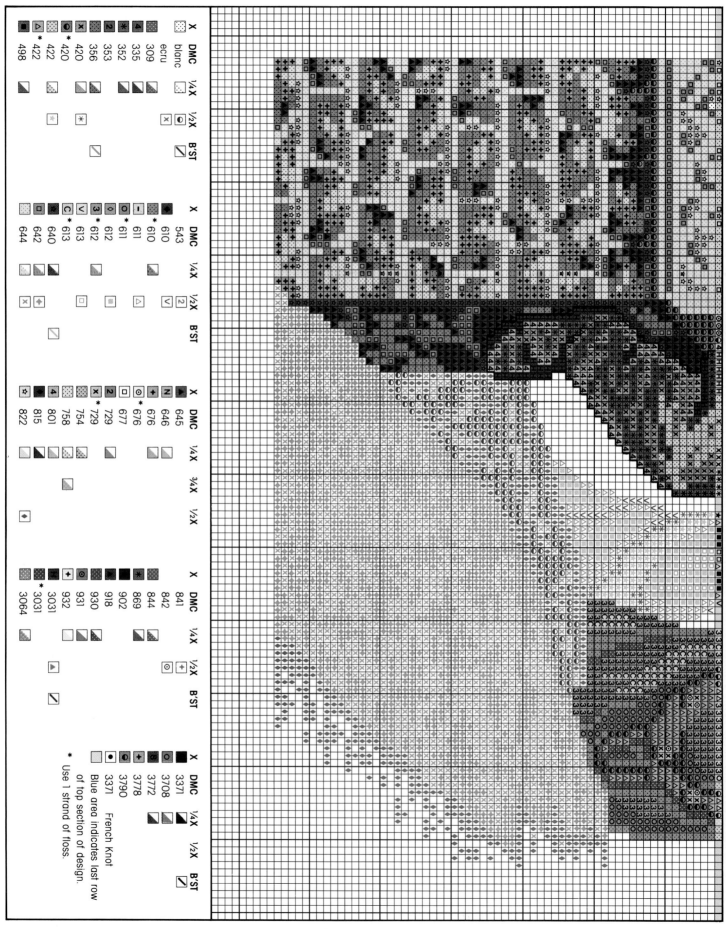

X	DMC	¼X	½X	B'ST
⬚	blanc	⬚		
▶	ecru	◩		
⬚	309			
⊞	335	◩		
⬚	352	◩		
◪	353	◩		
✳	356	◩		
◢	420			
⊠	420*	◩	⊠	◩
◯	422	◳		
▷	422*			
◼	498	◩		

X	DMC	¼X	½X	B'ST
⬚	543	◩	⊠	
⬚	610	◩	▷	
◼	610*	◼	◼	◩
◇	611	◩		
◯	611*			
▮	612	◩		
◆	612*	◳	◩	
✦	613			
◼	613*	◩	◩	
▨	640	◳	◳	
☑	642			
⬚	644	◳	▷	

X	DMC	¼X	¾X	½X	B'ST
✿	645	◩			
◼	646	◩			
▦	676	◩			
◯	676*				
⊠	677				
◧	729				
▨	729*				
⬚	754	◩			
◼	758	◩			
◼	801	◩			
◼	815	◩			
⬚	822	◩			

X	DMC	¼X	½X	B'ST
▨	841	◩		
▦	842	◩		
◼	844	◩		
✚	869	◩	▶	
◉	902			
◼	918	◩		
◼	930	◩		
◼	931	◩	◩	
◼	932		◯	
⊠	3031		✚	
▷	3031*	◆		
⬚	3064	◩	▶	◩

X	DMC	¼X	½X	B'ST
▨	3371	◩	◯	
◉	3708		✚	
◼	3772	◩		
◼	3778	◩		
◯	3790			
◼	3371	◩		◩

* French Knot

3790   Blue area indicates last row
of top section of design.

* Use 1 strand of floss.

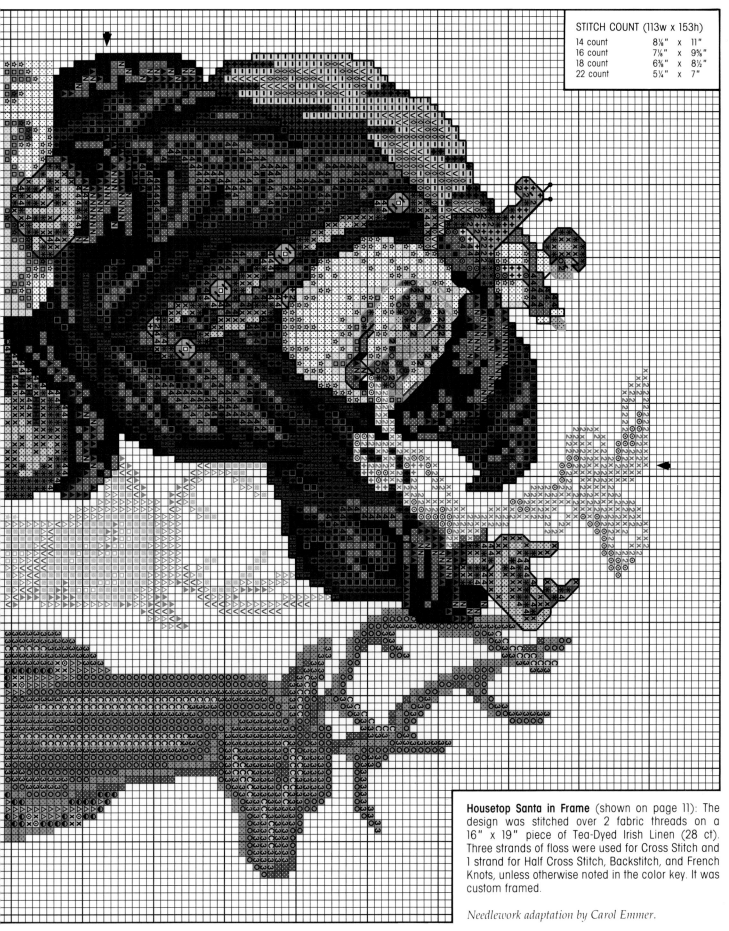

STITCH COUNT (113w x 153h)

14 count	8⅛"	x	11"
16 count	7⅛"	x	9⅝"
18 count	6⅜"	x	8½"
22 count	5¼"	x	7"

Housetop Santa in Frame (shown on page 11): The design was stitched over 2 fabric threads on a 16" x 19" piece of Tea-Dyed Irish Linen (28 ct). Three strands of floss were used for Cross Stitch and 1 strand for Half Cross Stitch, Backstitch, and French Knots, unless otherwise noted in the color key. It was custom framed.

Needlework adaptation by Carol Emmer.

all through the house

STITCH COUNT (83w x 91h)

14 count	6"	x	6½"
16 count	5¼"	x	5¾"
18 count	4⅝"	x	5⅛"
22 count	3⅞"	x	4¼"

Needlework adaptations by Donna Vermillion Giampa.

X	DMC	¼X	½X	B'ST		X	DMC	¼X		X	DMC	¼X	½X	B'ST		X	DMC	¼X	½X	B'ST		X	DMC	¼X	B'ST
	blanc					✳	469			▼	760					936					◨	3782		
	* blanc					C	471			✦	761					988					■	3790		⁄
	& 032					⊙	472			S	762					3031			⁄		S	† Kreinik	
◙	221					3	500			5	775					3032		✦			Fine Braid - 002
▲	312					◪	642			✦	781					3328					●	3031	French Knot
	319					◇	644			⊙	783					3347		⊙		* Use 3 strands of
	322					▢	676			2	822					3713					floss and 1 strand
	347					4	725			✦	926		⊙			C	3755				of Kreinik Blending
	356		⁄				729			H	927		▲				3773				Filament - 032.
-	368		★			△	754			V	928						3774				† Use 1 strand of
	451		✕			✭	758			▲	934		⁄			✦	3781		■		Fine Braid.

14 count	3¾"	x	5¾"
16 count	3¼"	x	5"
18 count	2⅞"	x	4½"
22 count	2⅜"	x	3⅝"

Blue Santa in Frame (shown on page 14): The design was stitched over 2 fabric threads on a 13" x 15" piece of Ivory Lugana (25 ct). Three strands of floss were used for Cross Stitch and 1 strand for Backstitch. Attach beads using 1 strand of DMC 498 floss. (See Attaching Beads, page 95.) It was custom framed.

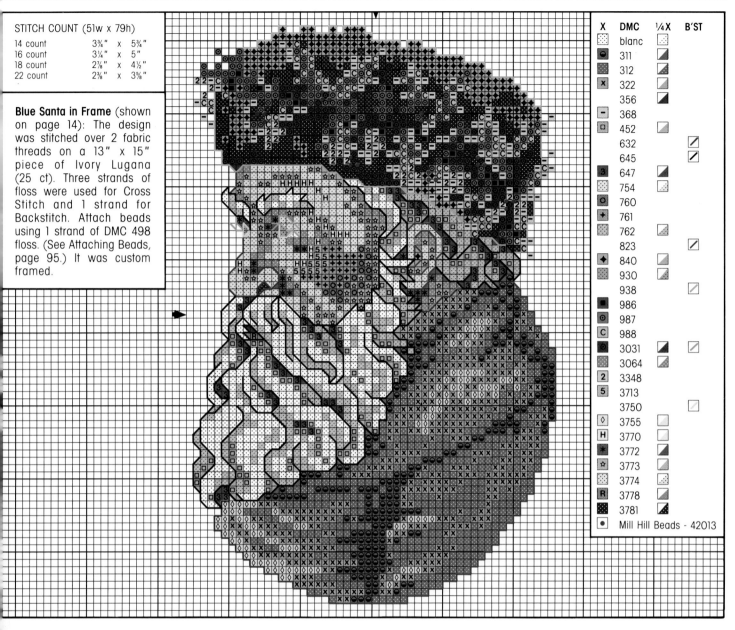

X	DMC	¼X	B'ST
	blanc		
⊙	311		
▨	312		
✕	322		
	356		
–	368		
□	452		
	632		╱
	645		╱
▩	647		
	754		
⊙	760		
+	761		
▨	762		
	823		╱
◆	840		
▨	930		
	938		╱
■	986		
⊙	987		
C	988		
▨	3031		╱
	3064		
2	3348		
5	3713		
	3750		╱
◇	3755		
H	3770		
✳	3772		
☆	3773		
▨	3774		
R	3778		
▨	3781		
•	Mill Hill Beads - 42013		

Santa at the Door Pillow (shown on page 12): The design was stitched over 2 fabric threads on a 15" x 16" piece of Ivory Lugana (25 ct). Three strands of floss were used for Cross Stitch and 1 strand for Half Cross Stitch, Backstitch, and French Knots, unless otherwise noted in color key.

For pillow, you will need an 8⅝" x 11" piece of fabric for lining stitched piece, two 16⅝" x 11" pieces of fabric for pillow front and backing, 2" x 22" bias strip of fabric for ¼" dia. cord, 2½" x 55¼" bias strip of fabric for ½" dia. cord, 22" length of ¼" dia. purchased cord, 55¼" length of ½" dia. purchased cord, and polyester fiberfill.

Centering design, trim stitched piece to measure 8⅝" x 11". Baste lining fabric to wrong side of stitched piece close to raw edges.

Center ¼" dia. cord on wrong side of bias strip; matching long edges, fold strip

over cord. Use a zipper foot to baste along length of strip close to cord; trim seam allowance to ½" and cut length of cording in half. Matching raw edges, baste one length of cording to right side of one long edge of stitched piece. Press seam allowance toward stitched piece. Repeat with remaining length of cord and long edge of stitched piece.

For pillow front, center wrong side of stitched piece on right side of one 16⅝" x 11" piece of fabric; baste in place. Using zipper foot and same color thread as cording, attach stitched piece to pillow front by sewing through all layers as close as possible to cording, taking care not to catch fabric of stitched piece.

Center ½" dia. cord on wrong side of bias strip; matching long edges, fold strip over cord. Baste along length of strip close to cord; trim seam allowance to ½". Matching raw edges, pin cording to right

side of pillow front making a ⅜" clip in seam allowance of cording at corners. Ends of cording should overlap approximately 2"; pin overlapping end out of the way. Starting 2" from beginning end of cording and ending 4" from overlapping end, baste cording to pillow front. On overlapping end of cording, remove 2½" of basting; fold end of fabric back and trim cord so that it meets beginning end of cord. Fold end of fabric under ½"; wrap fabric over beginning end of cording. Finish basting cording to pillow front.

Matching right sides and leaving an opening for turning, use a ½" seam allowance to sew pillow front and backing fabric together. Trim seam allowances diagonally at corners; turn pillow right side out carefully pushing corners outward. Stuff pillow with polyester fiberfill and blind stitch opening closed.

all through the house

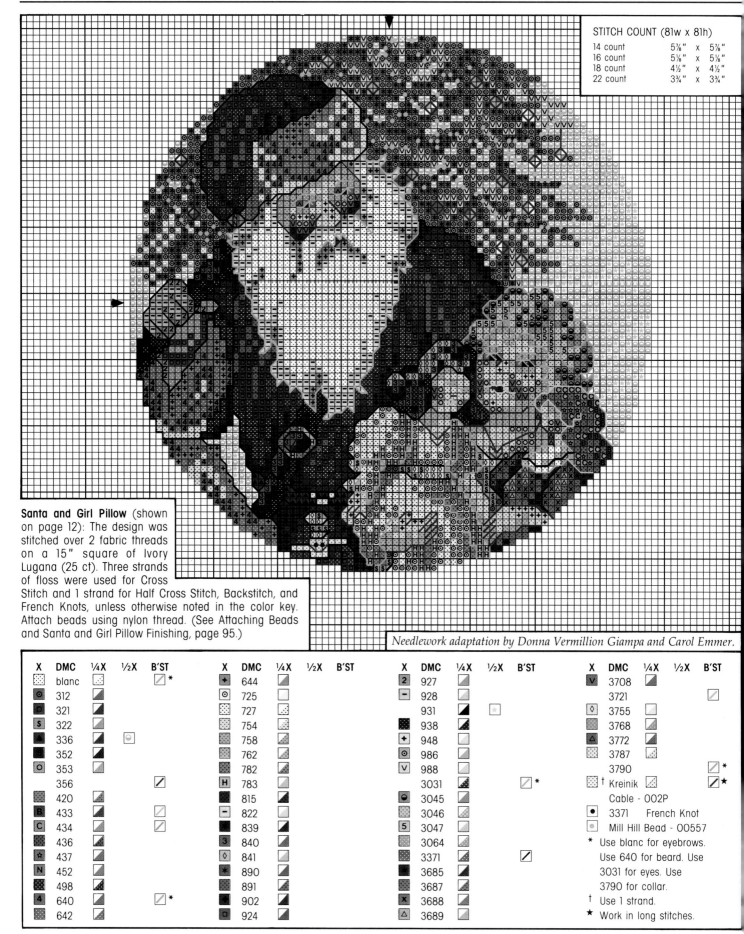

STITCH COUNT (81w x 81h)

14 count	5⅞"	x	5⅞"
16 count	5⅛"	x	5⅛"
18 count	4½"	x	4½"
22 count	3¾"	x	3¾"

Santa and Girl Pillow (shown on page 12): The design was stitched over 2 fabric threads on a 15" square of Ivory Lugana (25 ct). Three strands of floss were used for Cross Stitch and 1 strand for Half Cross Stitch, Backstitch, and French Knots, unless otherwise noted in the color key. Attach beads using nylon thread. (See Attaching Beads and Santa and Girl Pillow Finishing, page 95.)

Needlework adaptation by Donna Vermillion Giampa and Carol Emmer.

X	DMC	¼X	½X	B'ST		X	DMC	¼X	½X	B'ST		X	DMC	¼X	½X	B'ST		X	DMC	¼X	½X	B'ST
	blanc			✦ *		✦	644					2	927					V	3708			
⊙	312					⊙	725					–	928						3721			✦
◻	321						727						931		★			◇	3755			
S	322						754					▦	938						3768			
▲	336		⊙			H	758					✦	948					△	3772			
O	352						762					⊙	986						3787			
O	353						782					V	988						3790			✦ *
	356			✦		H	783						3031			✦ *		▦ †	Kreinik			✦ ★
	420						815					⊙	3045						Cable - 002P			
B	433			✦		–	822						3046					●	3371	French Knot		
C	434			✦		▮	839					5	3047					○	Mill Hill Bead - 00557			
	436					◇	840						3064					*	Use blanc for eyebrows.			
★	437					◇	841						3371			✦			Use 640 for beard. Use			
N	452					✦	890						3685						3031 for eyes. Use			
▦	498						891						3687						3790 for collar.			
4	640			✦ *		▮	902					X	3688					†	Use 1 strand.			
	642					⊡	924					△	3689					★	Work in long stitches.			

61 x 131 threads

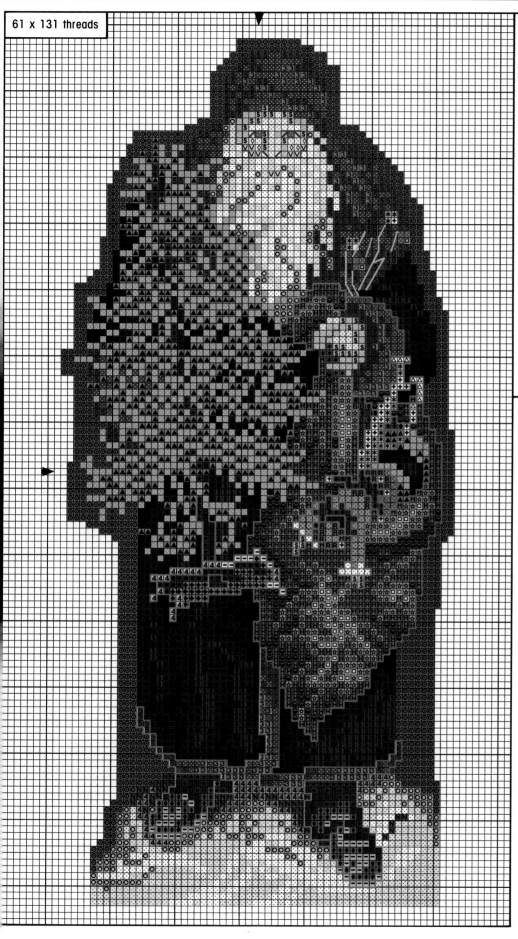

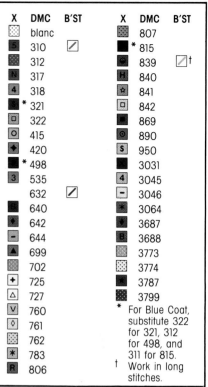

X	DMC	B'ST		X	DMC	B'ST
	blanc				807	
S	310	⟋		■	* 815	
	312			⊙	839	⟋ †
N	317			H	840	
4	318			✿	841	
■	* 321			□	842	
□	322			■	869	
O	415			⊙	890	
◆	420			S	950	
■	* 498			■	3031	
3	535			4	3045	
	632	⟋		-	3046	
	640			*	3064	
◆	642			◆	3687	
-	644			B	3688	
▲	699				3773	
	702				3774	
✦	725				3787	
△	727			R	3799	
V	760			*	For Blue Coat,	
◇	761				substitute 322	
	762				for 321, 312	
*	783				for 498, and	
R	806				311 for 815.	
				†	Work in long	
					stitches.	

Standing Santa Figures (shown on page 15) : The design was cross stitched on a 10½" x 13½" sheet of 10 mesh plastic canvas. Eight strands of floss were used for Cross Stitch and Overcast Stitch and 3 strands for Backstitch. (See Working With Plastic Canvas, page 95.)

For each standing figure, trim stitched piece leaving one unworked plastic canvas thread around design on all sides. You will also need a 10½" x 13½" sheet of 10 mesh plastic canvas for backing, a 7" x 5" piece of 10 mesh plastic canvas for base, aquarium gravel, plastic sandwich bag, and polyester fiberfill.

Trim backing to match stitched piece exactly. On **right side** of backing, use desired floss color to cross stitch entire piece, leaving one unworked plastic canvas thread around stitched area on all sides.

Matching wrong sides and leaving lower edge open for stuffing, use Overcast Stitch and desired floss color to join stitched piece and backing.

Stuff figure with polyester fiberfill to within 1½" of opening. Fill sandwich bag with a small amount of aquarium gravel and place into opening of figure.

Use Base Pattern (page 96) to cut base piece from plastic canvas (lines on pattern represent canvas threads). Use Overcast Stitch and desired floss color to join base to opening of figure.

Needlework adaptation by Donna Vermillion Giampa.

ST. NICK AFGHAN

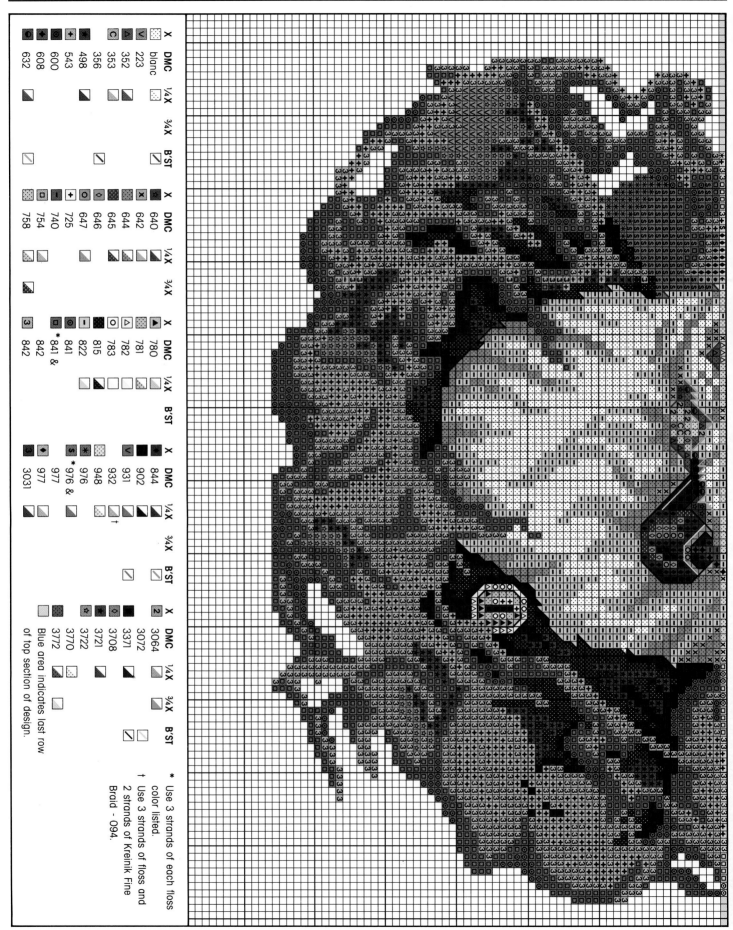

X							¼X				DMC
						C		△	∨		
											blanc
											223
											352
											353
											356
											498
											543
											600
											608
											632

¾X								
B'ST								

X									¼X				DMC
	□	I	+	○	◇		×						640
													642
													644
													645
													646
													647
													758
													754
													740
													725
													822
													815

¾X				

X					¼X					DMC
3	□	○	I		▶	△	○			780
										781
										782
										783
										842
										842
										*841 &
										841

B'ST					

X				¼X				DMC
3	◆	S	✴	∨	■			844
								902
								931
								932
								948
								3031
								977
								977
								*976 &
								976

¾X		
B'ST		

X					¼X				DMC
2		✿	✴	◇	■				3064
									3072
									3371
									3708
									3721
									3722
									3770
									3772

¾X		
B'ST		

Blue area indicates last row
of top section of design.

* Use 3 strands of each floss
color listed.
† Use 3 strands of floss and
2 strands of Kreinik Fine
Braid – 094.

64

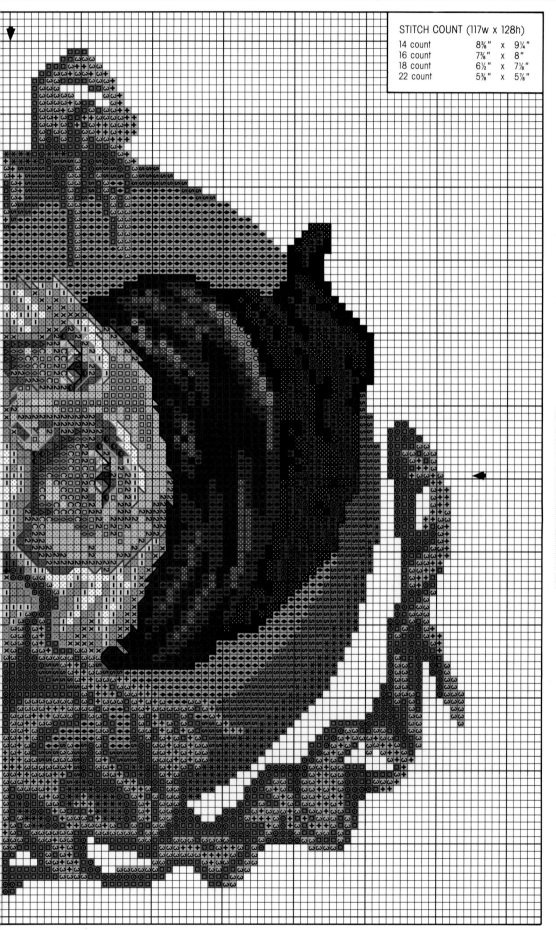

St. Nick Afghan (shown on page 17): The design was stitched over 2 fabric threads on a 45" x 58" piece of Bayberry Anne Cloth (18 ct).

For afghan, cut off selvages of fabric; measure 5½" from raw edge of fabric and pull out 1 fabric thread. Fringe fabric up to missing fabric thread. Repeat for each side. Tie an overhand knot at each corner with 4 horizontal and 4 vertical fabric threads. Working from corners, use 8 fabric threads for each knot until all threads are knotted.

Refer to Diagram for placement of design on fabric; use 6 strands of floss for Cross Stitch and 2 strands for Backstitch, unless otherwise noted in the color key.

Needlework adaptation by Carol Emmer.

Diagram

the children's friend

X	DMC	¼X	¾X	½X	B'ST
	blanc				∕ *
	309	∕			
	311				∕
	312	∕			
	319	∕			∕ *
△	320	∕			
	322	∕			
	335	∕			
	352	∕			
○	353	∕			
	356				∕
*	367	∕			
V	368				
	420	∕			
X	422				
	433	∕			∕ *
4	434	∕			∕
	436	∕			
	437	∕			
	498	∕			
	610	∕			
	611	∕			
	612	∕			
◇	613	∕			
	632				∕ †
	640				∕
	642	∕			
2	644	∕			
	676			−	
	677			★	
	680			▲	
X	725				
	729			◑	
△	738	∕			
−	754				
3	758	∕	∕		
C	775				
▲	782				
★	782	∕			
	783				
☆ ★	783				∕ † ★
S	801	∕			
	815	∕			
	822				
	869	∕			
◉	890	∕			∕ *
	899				
	902	∕			
	938				∕
	948				
	3031	∕			∕ †
	3064	∕	∕		
☆	3325	∕			
□	3326	∕			
◉	3345	∕			
4	3346	∕			
✦	3347	∕			
○	3348	∕			
2	3708	∕			
	3721				∕ †

X	DMC	¼X	¾X	½X	B'ST
	3755	∕			
	3772	∕	∕		

Blue area indicates first row of right section of design.

* Use blanc for eyebrows. Use 319 for letters and holly. Use 433 for hair and box. Use 890 for boy's shirt.

† Use 632 for nose. Use 783 for banner. Use 3031 for eyes. Use 3721 for lips and box.

★ Add 1 strand of Kreinik Blending Filament - 002.

CHRISTMAS·TO·YOU

A Merry Christmas to You in Frame (shown on page 19): The design was stitched over 2 fabric threads on a 23" x 14" piece of Cream Belfast Linen (32 ct). Two strands of floss were used for Cross Stitch and 1 strand for Half Cross Stitch and Backstitch, unless otherwise noted in the color key. It was custom framed.

Needlework adaptation by Carol Emmer.

a christmas welcome

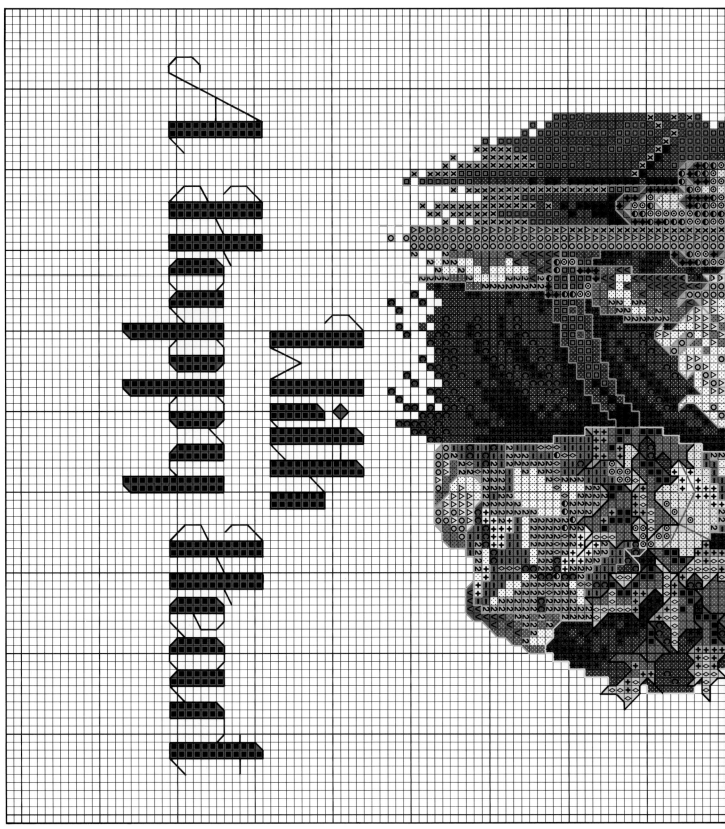

Enter with a Happy Heart Banner (shown on page 20): The design was stitched over 2 fabric threads on a 21" x 38" piece of Cracked Wheat Ragusa (14 ct). Six strands of floss were used for Cross Stitch and 2 strands for Backstitch, unless otherwise noted in the color key.

Center design horizontally and stitch with top of design 7½" from one short edge of fabric. Measure 2" from bottom of design and pull out one horizontal fabric thread. Fringe up to missing fabric thread. On each long edge turn fabric ½" to wrong side and press; turn ½" wrong side again and hem. Trim fringe to 3". For casing at top edge turn fabric ½" to wrong side and press; turn 2" to wrong side again and hem. Insert rod in casing.

Needlework adaptation by Donna Vermillion Giampa and Carol Emmer.

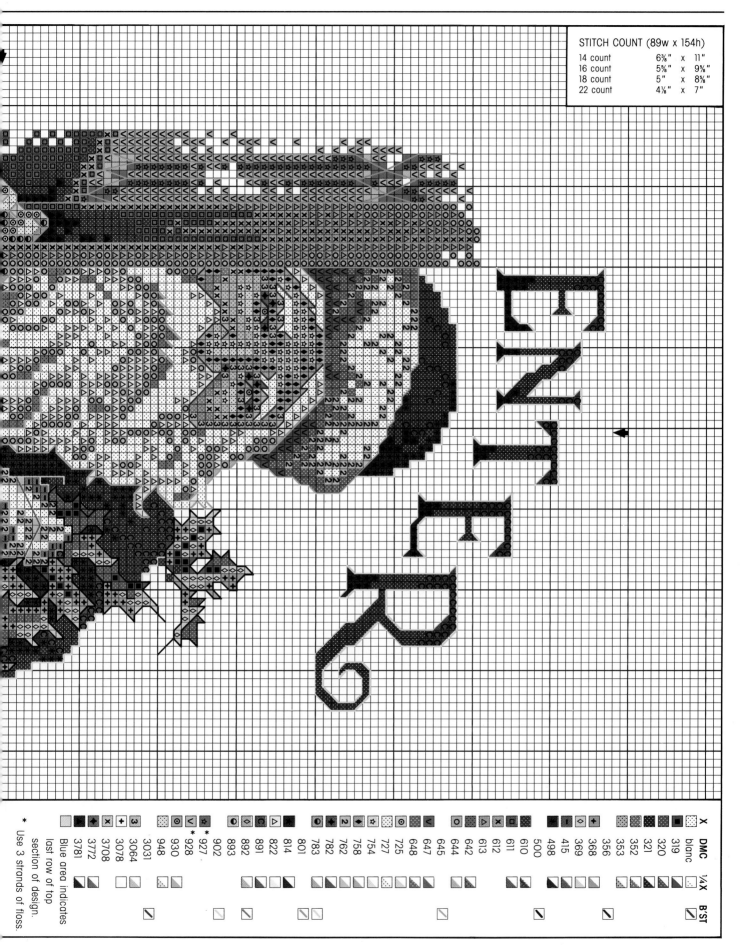

STITCH COUNT (89w x 154h)

14 count	6⅜" x	11"
16 count	5⅝" x	9⅝"
18 count	5" x	8⅝"
22 count	4⅛" x	7"

*
Use 3 strands of floss.

section of design.
last row of top
Blue area indicates

X	DMC	¼X	B'ST
	blanc		
	319		
	320		
	321		
	352		
	353		
	356		
	368		
	369		
	415		
	498		
	500		
	610		
	611		
	612		
	613		
	642		
	644		
	645		
	647		
	648		
	725		
	727		
	754		
	758		
	762		
	782		
	783		
	801		
	814		
	822		
	891		
	892		
	893		
	902		
	927		
	928		
	930		
	948		
	3031		
	3064		
	3078		
	3708		
	3772		
	3781		

69

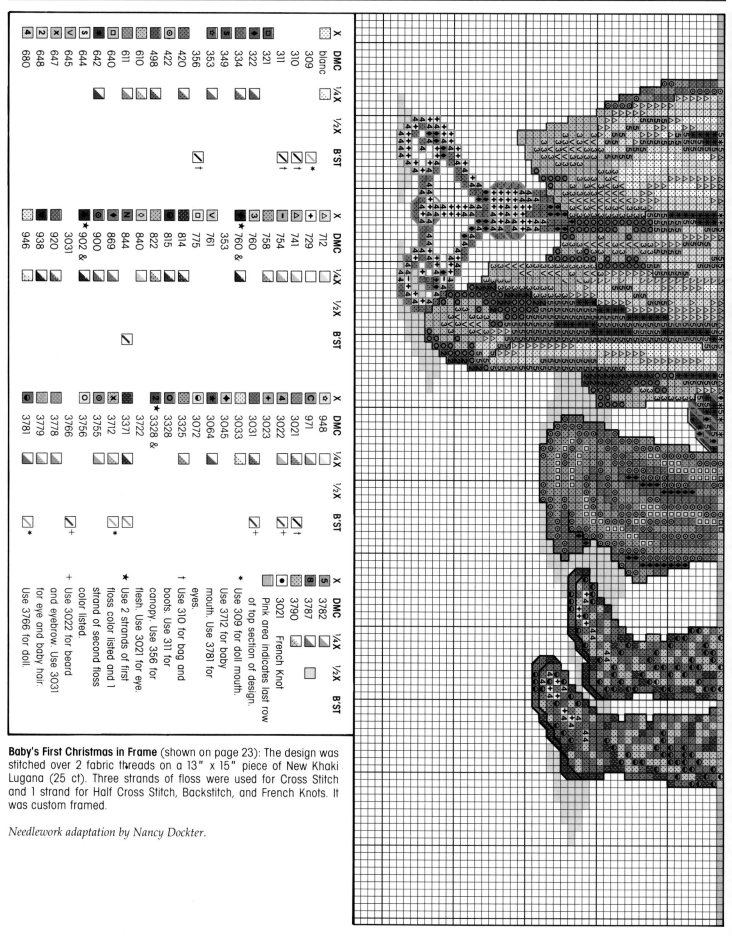

Color Key (DMC):

X	¼X	½X	B'ST	DMC
				blanc
				309
				310
				311
				321
				322
				334
				349
				353
				356
				420
				422
				498
				610
				611
				640
				642
				644
				645
				647
				648
				680

X	¼X	½X	B'ST	DMC
				712
				729
				741
				754
				758
				760
				760 &
				761
				775
				814
				815
				822
				840
				844
				869
				900
				902 &
				920
				938
				946
				3031

X	¼X	½X	B'ST	DMC
				948
				971
				3021
				3022
				3023
				3031
				3033
				3045
				3064
				3072
				3325
				3328
				3328 &
				3371
				3712
				3722
				3755
				3756
				3766
				3778
				3779
				3781

X	¼X	½X	B'ST	DMC
				3782
				3787
				3790
				3021

French Knot

Pink area indicates last row of top section of design.

* Use 309 for doll mouth. Use 3712 for baby mouth. Use 3781 for eyes.

† Use 310 for bag and boots. Use 311 for canopy. Use 356 for flesh. Use 3021 for eye.

★ Use 2 strands of first floss color listed and 1 strand of second floss color listed.

+ Use 3022 for beard and eyebrow. Use 3031 for eye and baby hair. Use 3766 for doll.

Baby's First Christmas in Frame (shown on page 23): The design was stitched over 2 fabric threads on a 13" x 15" piece of New Khaki Lugana (25 ct). Three strands of floss were used for Cross Stitch and 1 strand for Half Cross Stitch, Backstitch, and French Knots. It was custom framed.

Needlework adaptation by Nancy Dockter.

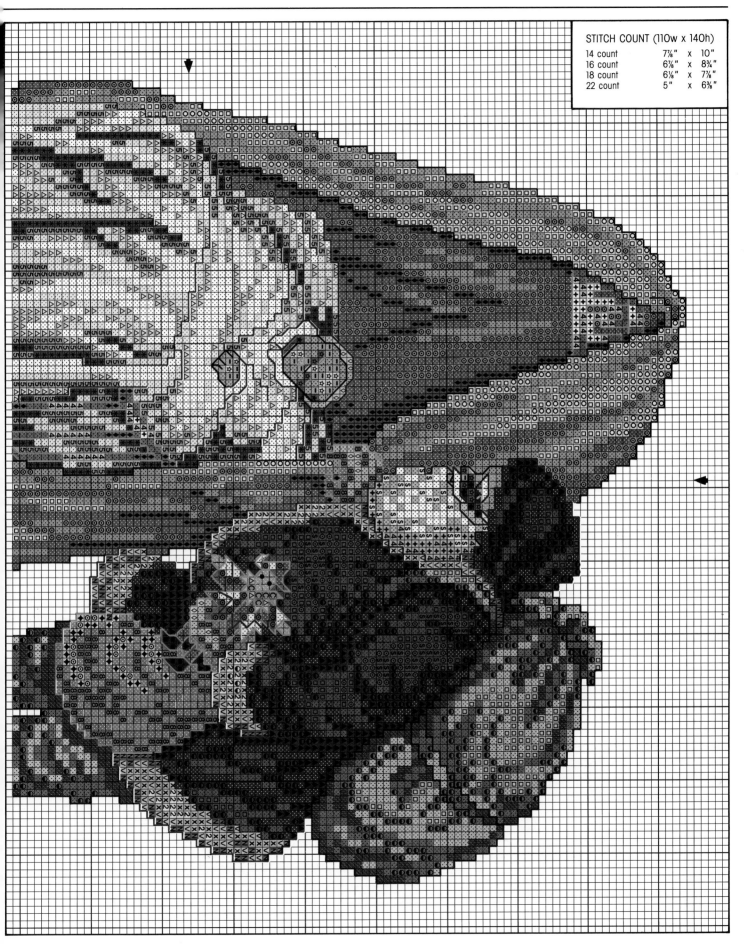

STITCH COUNT (110w x 140h)

count		
14 count	7⅞"	x 10"
16 count	6⅞"	x 8¾"
18 count	6⅛"	x 7⅞"
22 count	5"	x 6⅜"

MEMORY ALBUM

STITCH COUNT (63w x 105h)

count			
14 count	4½"	x	7½"
16 count	4"	x	6⅝"
18 count	3½"	x	5⅞"
22 count	2⅞"	x	4⅞"

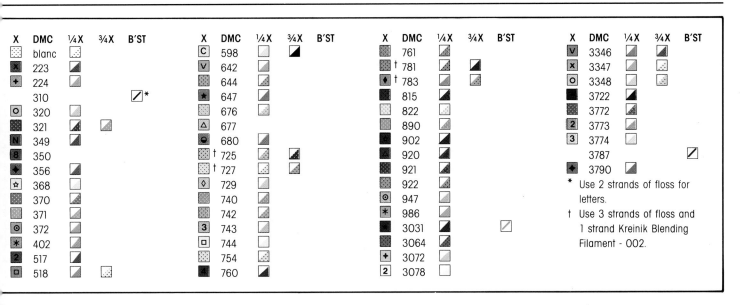

X	DMC	¼X	¾X	B'ST	X	DMC	¼X	¾X	B'ST	X	DMC	¼X	¾X	B'ST	X	DMC	¼X	¾X	B'ST
	blanc	✓			C	598	✓	✓			761	✓			V	3346	✓	✓	
✳	223	✓			V	642	✓				† 781	✓	✓		x	3347	✓	✓	
✛	224	✓				644	✓			♦	† 783	✓			o	3348	✓		
	310			✓*	★	647					815					3722	✓		
o	320	✓				676	✓				822	✓				3772	✓		
	321	✓	✓		△	677	✓				890				2	3773	✓		
N	349	✓			⊙	680	✓				902				3	3774			
8	350	✓				† 725	✓	✓			920	✓				3787			✓
✦	356	✓				† 727	✓	✓			921	✓			♦	3790	✓		
☆	368				◊	729	✓				922	✓							
	370	✓				740	✓			⊙	947	✓							
	371					742	✓			✳	986	✓							
⊙	372	✓			3	743	✓				3031	✓		✓					
✳	402	✓			□	744					3064	✓							
2	517	✓				754	✓			✛	3072								
□	518	✓	✓			760	✓			2	3078								

* Use 2 strands of floss for letters.

† Use 3 strands of floss and 1 strand Kreinik Blending Filament - 002.

Christmas Memories Album Cover (shown on page 25): The design was stitched over 2 fabric threads on a 13" x 17" piece of black Lugana (25 ct). Three strands of floss were used for Cross Stitch and 1 strand for Backstitch, unless otherwise noted in the color key.

With design centered, trim stitched piece to measure 8" x 11¼". For album, you will need a 10¼"w x 12"h photo album with a ¾" spine, 1 yard of 44"w fabric, 22" x 12" piece of batting for album, 6" x 9¼" piece of batting for stitched piece, two 5½" x 11½" pieces of poster board, 6" x 9¼" piece of mounting board, 32" length of ¼" dia. metallic gold cord, 13" length of ¼" dia. metallic gold double tasseled cord, and thick clear-drying craft glue.

Cut two 3" x 12" strips of fabric. Glue one long edge of one strip ¼" under one long side of metal spine inside album; glue remaining edges of strip to album. Repeat with remaining strip and long side of metal spine; allow to dry.

Glue batting to outside of album. Cut a 24" x 14" piece of fabric for outside of album. Center album, batting side down, on wrong side of fabric; fold fabric at corners to inside of album and glue in place. At center bottom of album, turn a 4" section of fabric ¼" to wrong side (**Fig. 1**); glue folded edge under spine of album. Repeat at center top of album. Fold remaining edges of fabric to inside of album and glue in place; allow to dry.

Fig. 1

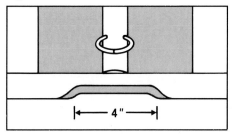

Cut two 11½" x 13½" pieces of fabric for inside covers. Center one piece of poster board on wrong side of one piece of fabric; fold edges of fabric to back of poster board and glue in place. Glue wrong side of covered poster board to inside of front cover of album approximately ¼" from top, bottom, and outside edge of album. Repeat with remaining piece of fabric and poster board for inside back cover.

To mount stitched piece, glue batting to mounting board. Center stitched piece on batting and fold edges of stitched piece to back of mounting board; glue in place. Center and glue wrong side of mounted stitched piece to front cover.

Beginning at center bottom of stitched piece glue metallic gold cord around outside edge of stitched piece, trim overlapping end to meet beginning end. Tie tasseled cord in a bow and glue to center bottom of stitched piece.

Needlework adaptation by Nancy Dockter and Donna Vermillion Giampa.

AN ALL-AMERICAN CELEBRATION

X	DMC	¼X	B'ST	X	DMC	¼X	B'ST
	blanc		☑	◉	729		
-	ecru			○	754		
	312	◣		5	758		◣
◆	319			✦	815		
○	320			☆	822		
▣	321			✴	844		◩
▲	322			✳	890		
4	334			✱	902		
◕	336			◼	939		
X	352	◣	☑	C	3031		☑
◇	353	◣		◇	3032		
	356		◹	X	3033		
2	367				3064		◩
V	368			-	3325		
✶	420			B	3371	◣	☑
R	498			◉	3705		
✻	640		☑	◉	3708		◩
N	642			C	3755		
▦	644	◳		◼	3781		
S	645			▨	3782		◩
✚	646			◼	3790		
4	647			◌	Mill Hill Bead		
C	676				Blue area indicates		
△	677				first row of right		
3	680				section of design.		

Patriotic Santa Afghan (shown on page 29): The design (omitting the border and adding snowflakes as desired) was stitched over 2 fabric threads on a 45" x 58" piece of Royal Blue Anne Cloth (18 ct).

For afghan, cut off selvages of fabric; measure 5½" from raw edge of fabric and pull out 1 fabric thread. Fringe fabric up to missing fabric thread. Repeat for each side. Tie an overhand knot at each corner with 4 horizontal and 4 vertical fabric threads. Working from corners, use 8 fabric threads for each knot until all threads are knotted.

Refer to Diagram for placement of design on fabric; use 6 strands of floss for Cross Stitch and 2 strands for Backstitch.

For reins, use Kreinik Fine Braid - 002 and begin at bead placement on bridles; refer to photo and tack in place as needed with nylon thread. Attach Mill Hill Pebble Beads - 05557 using 2 strands of DMC 498 floss. (See Attaching Beads, page 95.)

Diagram

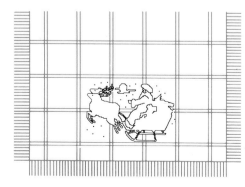

Patriotic Santa in Frame (shown on page 27): The design was stitched over 2 fabric threads on an 18" x 15" piece of Cream Belfast Linen (32 ct). Two strands of floss were used for Cross Stitch and 1 strand for Backstitch.

For reins, use Kreinik Cable - 002 and begin at bead placement on bridles; refer to photo and tack in place as needed with nylon thread. Attach Mill Hill Seed Beads - 00557 using 1 strand of DMC 498 floss. (See Attaching Beads, page 95.)

Needlework adaptation by Carol Emmer.

STITCH COUNT (161w x 100h)

14 count	11½"	x	7¼"
16 count	10⅛"	x	6¼"
18 count	9"	x	5⅝"
22 count	7⅜"	x	4⅝"

AN ALL-AMERICAN CELEBRATION

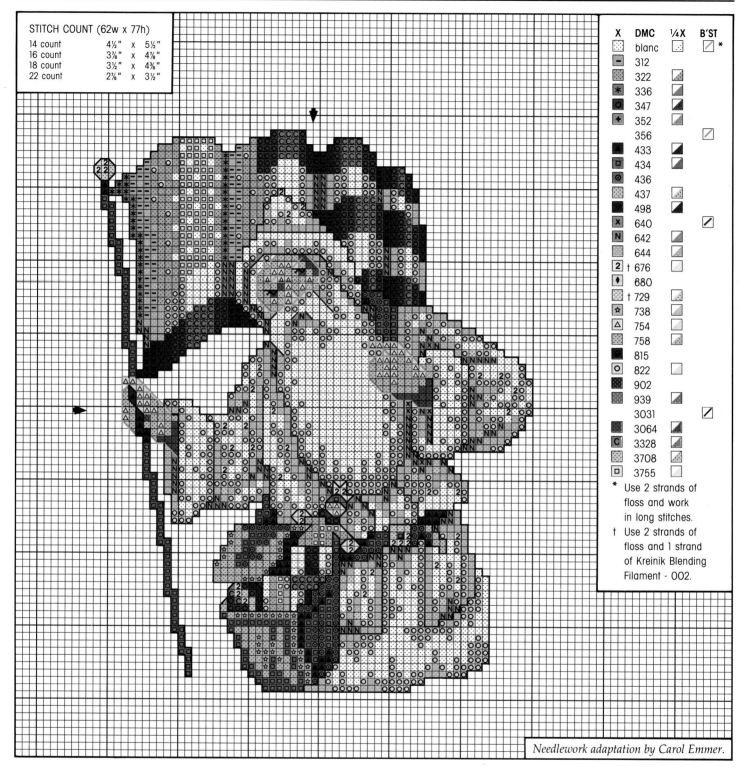

STITCH COUNT (62w x 77h)

14 count	4½"	x	5½"
16 count	3⅞"	x	4⅞"
18 count	3½"	x	4⅜"
22 count	2⅞"	x	3½"

X	DMC	¼X	B'ST
	blanc		◢ *
-	312		
	322	◥	
*	336	◥	
◉	347	◥	
✦	352	◥	
	356		◢
◼	433	◥	
▣	434	◥	
◎	436		
	437	◥	
◼	498	◥	
X	640		◢
N	642	◥	
	644	◥	
2	† 676	◻	
◆	680		
	† 729	◥	
☆	738	◥	
△	754	◥	
	758	◥	
◼	815		
O	822		
▨	902		
	939	◥	
	3031		◢
◼	3064	◥	
C	3328	◥	
	3708	◥	
◻	3755	◻	

* Use 2 strands of floss and work in long stitches.

† Use 2 strands of floss and 1 strand of Kreinik Blending Filament - 002.

Needlework adaptation by Carol Emmer.

Flag-Bearing Santa Ornaments (shown on page 28): Each design was stitched on a 13" square of Antique White Aida (16 ct). Two strands of floss were used for Cross Stitch and 1 strand for Backstitch, unless otherwise noted in the color key. They were stiffened and made into ornaments.

For each ornament, you will need a 13" square of lightweight cream fabric for backing, 30" length of jute, clear-drying craft glue, fabric stiffener, and small foam brush.

Follow Stiffening Instructions to stiffen each design. Fold length of jute in half and refer to photo to glue folded end to back of stiffened design. Refer to photo to tie ends of jute in a bow.

STIFFENING INSTRUCTIONS

Apply a heavy coat of fabric stiffener to back of stitched piece using small foam brush. Matching wrong sides, place stitched piece on backing fabric, smoothing stitched piece while pressing fabric pieces together; allow to dry. Apply fabric stiffener to backing fabric; allow to dry. Cut out close to edges of stitched design.

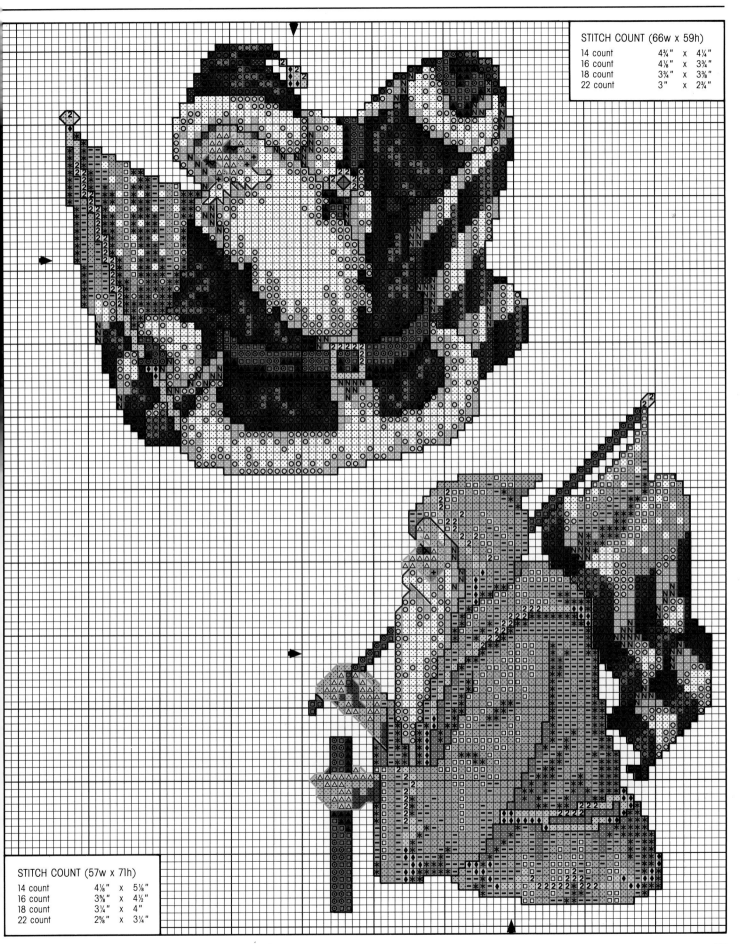

STITCH COUNT (66w x 59h)

14 count	4¾"	x 4¼"
16 count	4⅛"	x 3¾"
18 count	3¾"	x 3⅜"
22 count	3"	x 2¾"

STITCH COUNT (57w x 71h)

14 count	4⅛"	x 5⅛"
16 count	3⅝"	x 4½"
18 count	3¼"	x 4"
22 count	2⅝"	x 3¼"

HANDSOME TREE SKIRT

STITCH COUNT (71w x 94h)

count			
14 count	5⅛"	x	6¾"
16 count	4½"	x	5⅞"
18 count	4"	x	5¼"
22 count	3¼"	x	4⅜"

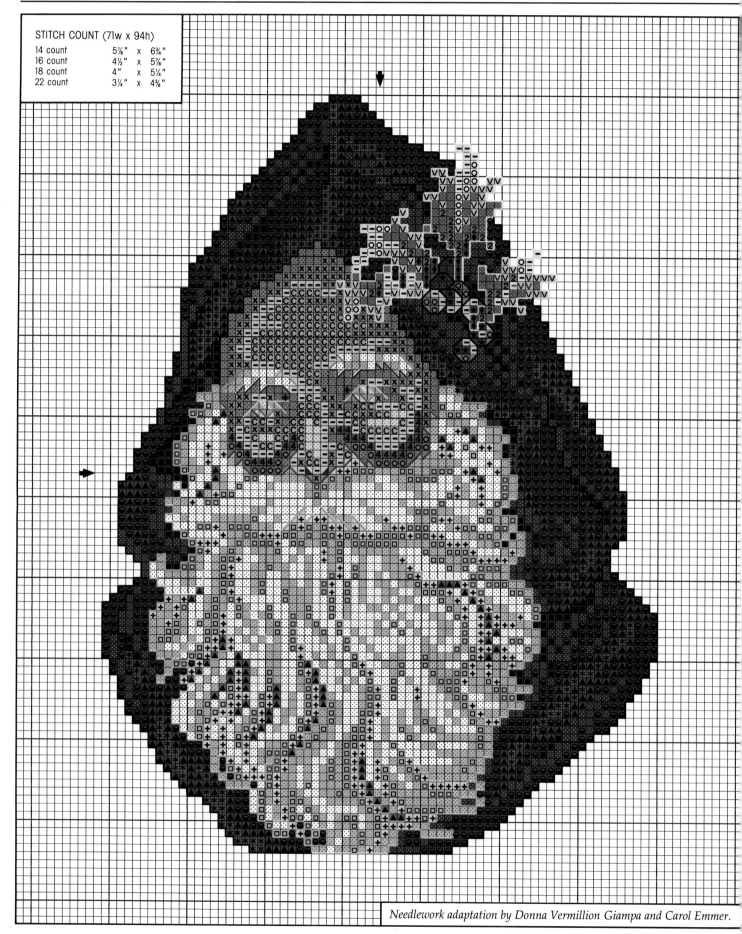

Needlework adaptation by Donna Vermillion Giampa and Carol Emmer.

X	DMC	¼X	¾X	B'ST
▨	blanc	▫		◪
●	321			
■	347	◪		
✦	351	◪		
◎	352	◪		
▬	353	◪		
	356			◪
◻	453	◪		
▨	498	◪		
◆	632			◪
	645			◪
▲	647			
✚	648	◪		
C	754	◪		
✕	758	◪	◪	
▨	762	◪		
■	814	◪		
▲	891			
✱	893			
	930			◪
	931	◪		
◆	934	◪		◪
2	937			
▨	948	◪		◪*
▨	3031			◪
▨	3064	◪		
■	3345			
V	3346	◪		
◎	3347			
▬	3348			
	3371			◪
◢	3708			
▨	3772	◪		

* Use 2 strands of floss.

Hooded Santa Pillow (shown on page 13): The design was stitched over 2 fabric threads on a 14" x 16" piece of Ivory Lugana (25 ct). Three strands of floss were used for Cross Stitch and 1 strand for Backstitch, unless otherwise noted in the color key. (See Hooded Santa Pillow Finishing, page 95.)

Handsome Tree Skirt (shown on page 31): The design was stitched over an 11" x 14" piece of 10 mesh waste canvas in one corner of a 45" square of wool fabric. Five strands of floss were used for Cross Stitch and 2 strands for Backstitch. (See Tree Skirt Finishing below.)

WORKING ON WASTE CANVAS

Waste canvas is a special canvas that provides an evenweave grid for placing stitches on fabric. After the design is worked over the canvas, the canvas threads are removed leaving the design on the fabric. The canvas is available in several mesh sizes.

Cover edges of canvas with masking tape. Cut a piece of lightweight, non-fusible interfacing the same size as canvas to provide a firm stitching base.

Find desired stitching area and mark center of area with a pin. Match center of canvas to pin. Pin canvas to fabric. Pin interfacing to wrong side of fabric. Baste all layers together as shown in **Fig. 1**.

Using a sharp needle, work design, stitching from large holes to large holes. Trim canvas to within ¾" of design. Dampen canvas until it becomes limp. Pull out canvas threads one at a time using tweezers (**Fig. 2**). Trim interfacing close to design.

Fig. 1   Fig. 2

TREE SKIRT FINISHING

For tree skirt, you will need a 5" length of string, thumbtack, and fabric marking pencil.

For fringe, machine stitch 3" away from all four edges of fabric. Fringe fabric to machine-stitched lines.

Fold fabric in half from top to bottom and again from left to right. To mark center opening cutting line, tie one end of string to fabric marking pencil. Insert thumbtack through string 1½" from pencil. Insert thumbtack in fabric as shown in **Fig. 3** and mark one-fourth of a circle. Cut out fabric along drawn line through all thicknesses. For back opening of skirt, refer to **Fig. 4** to cut from outer edge of one corner to center opening as indicated by dashed line. Clip curves of center opening and turn all raw edges ¼" to wrong side and press; turn ¼" to wrong side again and hem.

Referring to **Fig. 4**, place the design diagonally in corner, opposite back opening, with the bottom of the design 6" away from the corner of the tree skirt.

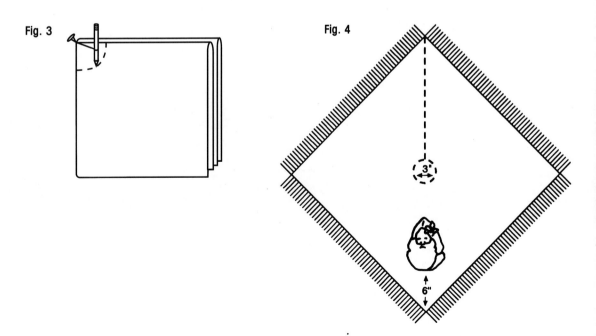

Fig. 3   Fig. 4

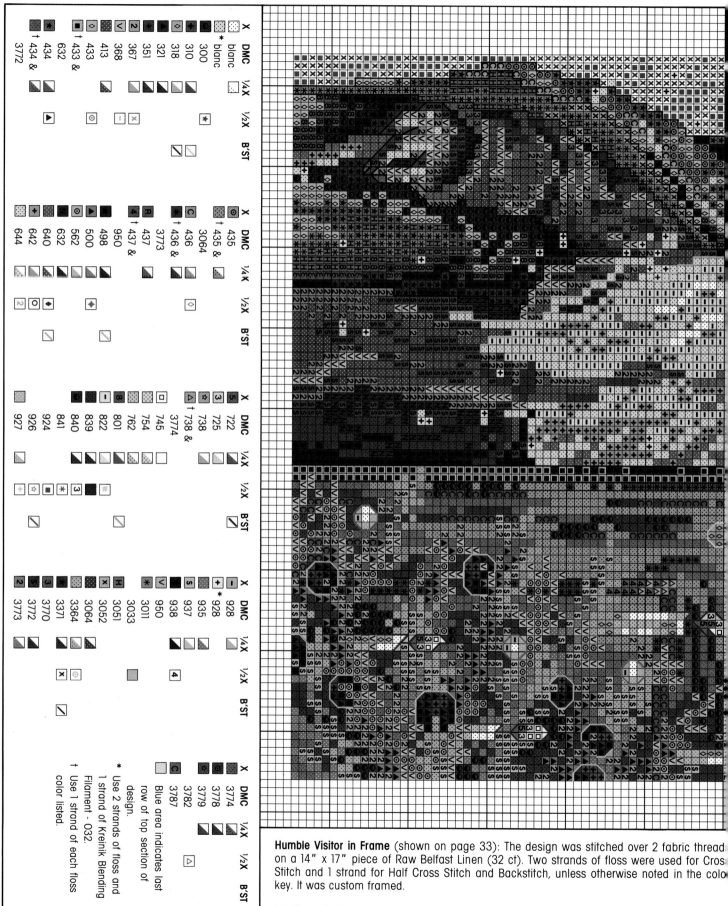

X	DMC	1/4X	1/2X	B'ST
	blanc			
	blanc *			
	300			
	310			
	318			
	321			
	351			
	367			
	368			
	413			
	433 &			
	433			
	434			
	434 &			
	632			
	3772			

X	DMC	1/4X	1/2X	B'ST
	435			
	435 &			
	436			
	436 &			
	437			
	437 &			
	498			
	500			
	562			
	632			
	640			
	642			
	644			
	950			
	3064			
	3773			

X	DMC	1/4X	1/2X	B'ST
	722			
	725			
	738 &			
	738			
	745			
	754			
	762			
	801			
	822			
	839			
	840			
	841			
	924			
	926			
	927			
	3774			

X	DMC	1/4X	1/2X	B'ST
	928			
	928 *			
	935			
	937			
	938			
	950			
	3011			
	3033			
	3051			
	3052			
	3064			
	3331			
	3364			
	3370			
	3772			
	3773			

X	DMC	1/4X	1/2X	B'ST
	3774			
	3778			
	3779			
	3782			
	3787			

* Use 2 strands of floss and
1 strand of Kreinik Blending
Filament - 032.

† Use 1 strand of each floss
color listed.

Blue area indicates last
row of top section of
design.

Humble Visitor in Frame (shown on page 33): The design was stitched over 2 fabric threads on a 14" x 17" piece of Raw Belfast Linen (32 ct). Two strands of floss were used for Cross Stitch and 1 strand for Half Cross Stitch and Backstitch, unless otherwise noted in the color key. It was custom framed.

Needlework adaptation by Nancy Dockter.

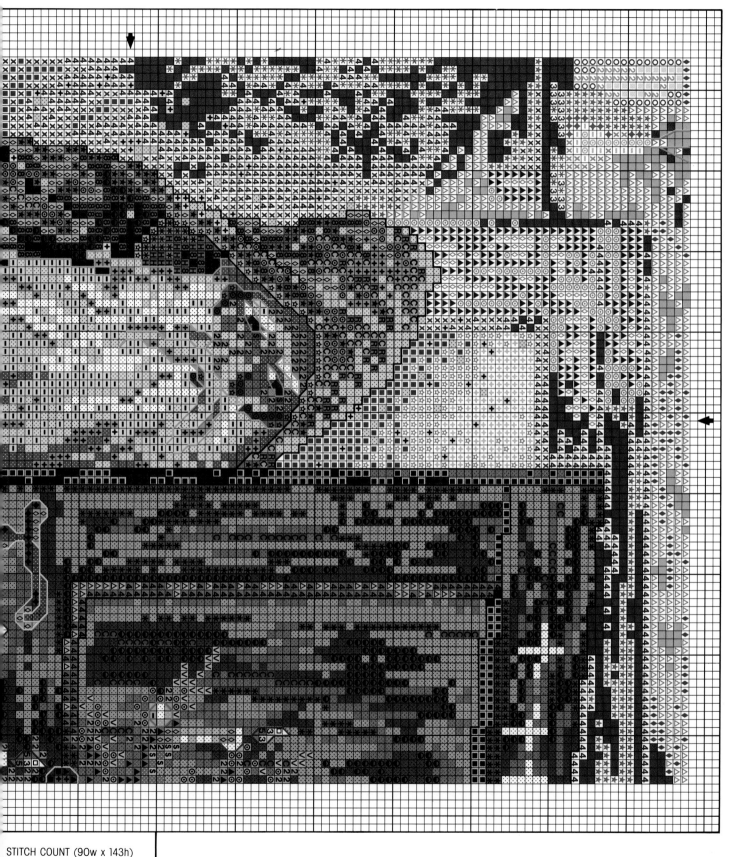

STITCH COUNT (90w x 143h)

14 count	6½"	x	10¼"
16 count	5⅝"	x	9"
18 count	5"	x	8"
22 count	4⅛"	x	6½"

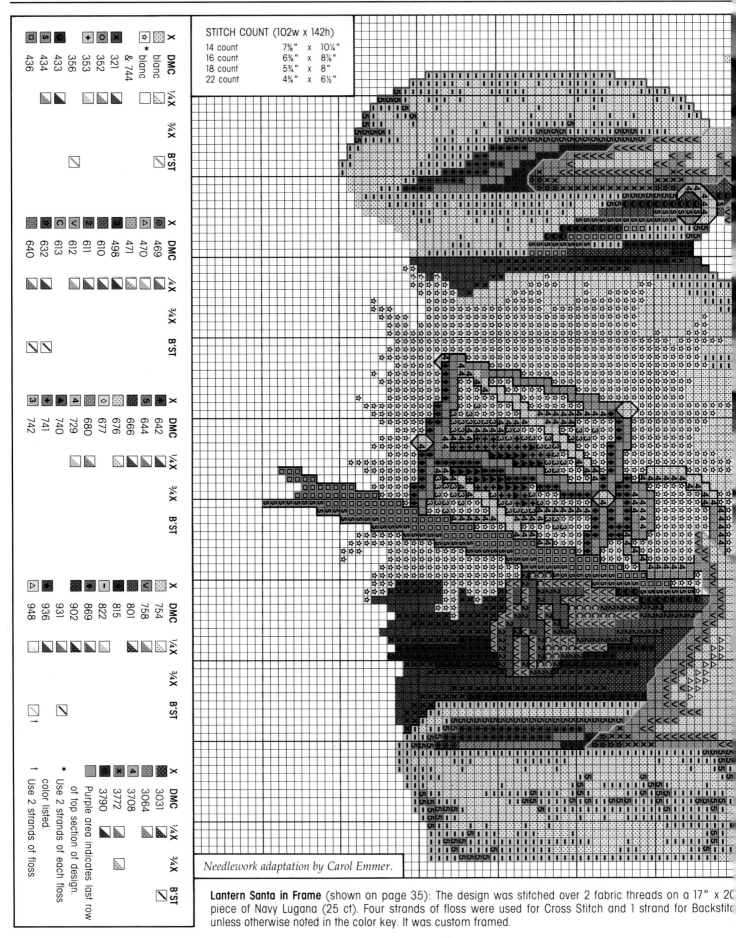

STITCH COUNT (102w x 142h)

14 count	7⅜"	x 10¼"
16 count	6⅜"	x 8⅞"
18 count	5¾"	x 8"
22 count	4¾"	x 6½"

Needlework adaptation by Carol Emmer.

Lantern Santa in Frame (shown on page 35): The design was stitched over 2 fabric threads on a 17" x 20" piece of Navy Lugana (25 ct). Four strands of floss were used for Cross Stitch and 1 strand for Backstitch unless otherwise noted in the color key. It was custom framed.

Purple area indicates last row of top section of design.

* Use 2 strands of each floss color listed.
† Use 2 strands of floss.

X / ¼X / ¾X / B'ST / DMC

blanc & 744
blanc
321
352
353
356
433
434
436

469
470
471
498
610
611
612
613
632
640

642
644
666
676
677
680
729
740
741
742

754
758
801
815
822
869
902
931
936
948

3031
3064
3708
3772
3790

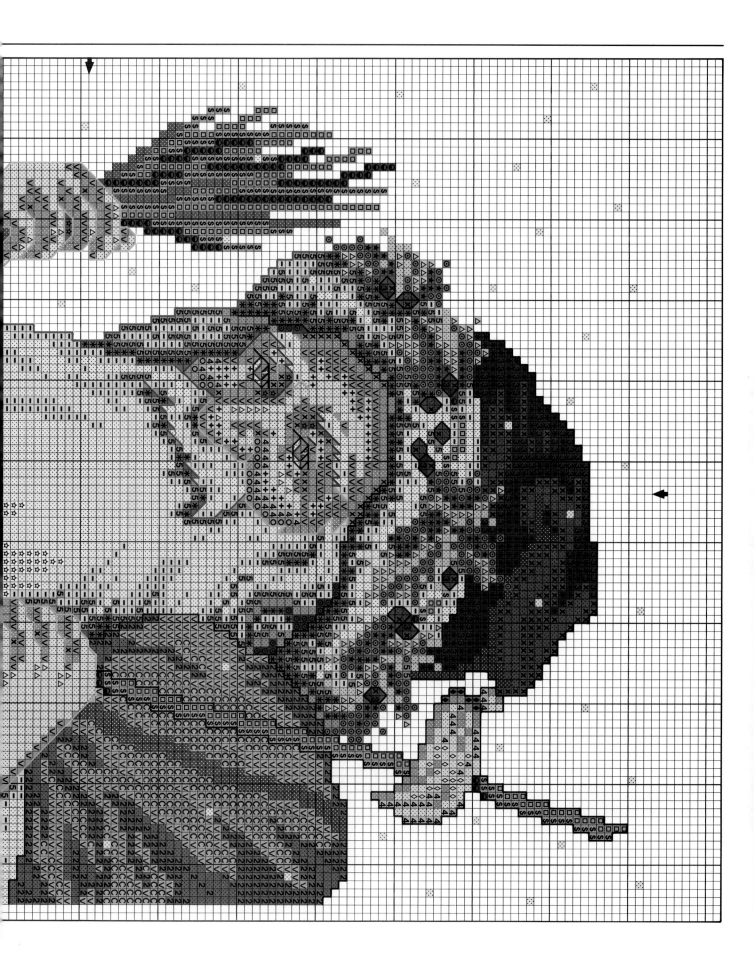

CHRISTMAS TRAVELER

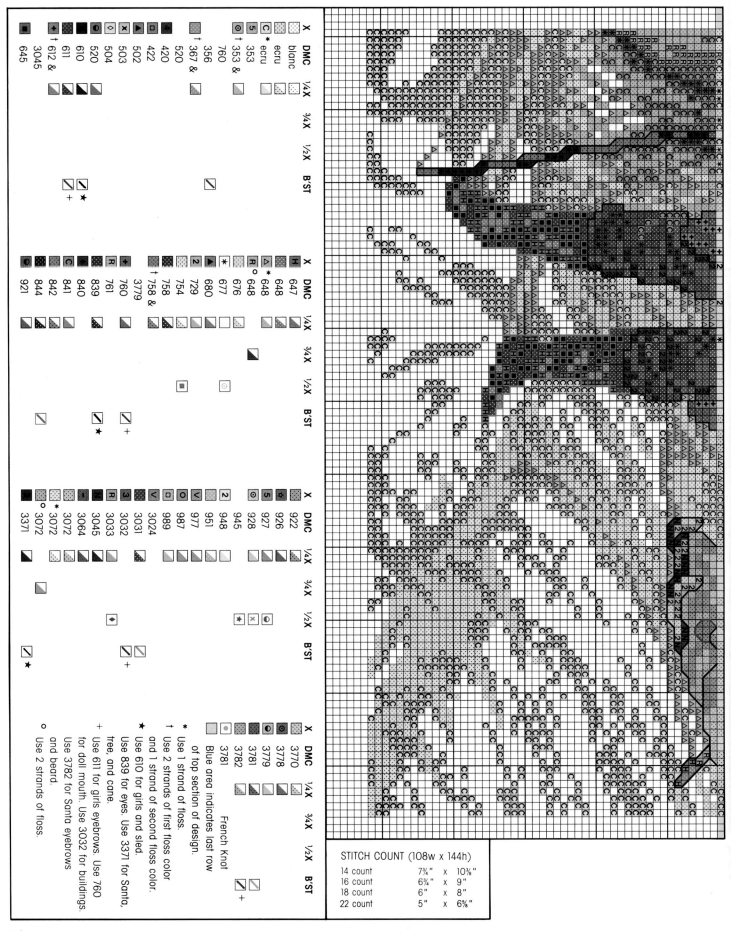

French Knot

Blue area indicates last row of top section of design.

* Use 1 strand of floss.
† Use 2 strands of first floss color and 1 strand of second floss color.
★ Use 610 for girls and sled. Use 839 for eyes. Use 3371 for tree, and cane.
+ Use 611 for girls eyebrows. Use 760 for doll mouth. Use 3032 for buildings. Use 3782 for Santa eyebrows and beard.
o Use 2 strands of floss.

STITCH COUNT (108w x 144h)		
14 count	7¾"	x 10⅜"
16 count	6¾"	x 9"
18 count	6"	x 8"
22 count	5"	x 6⅝"

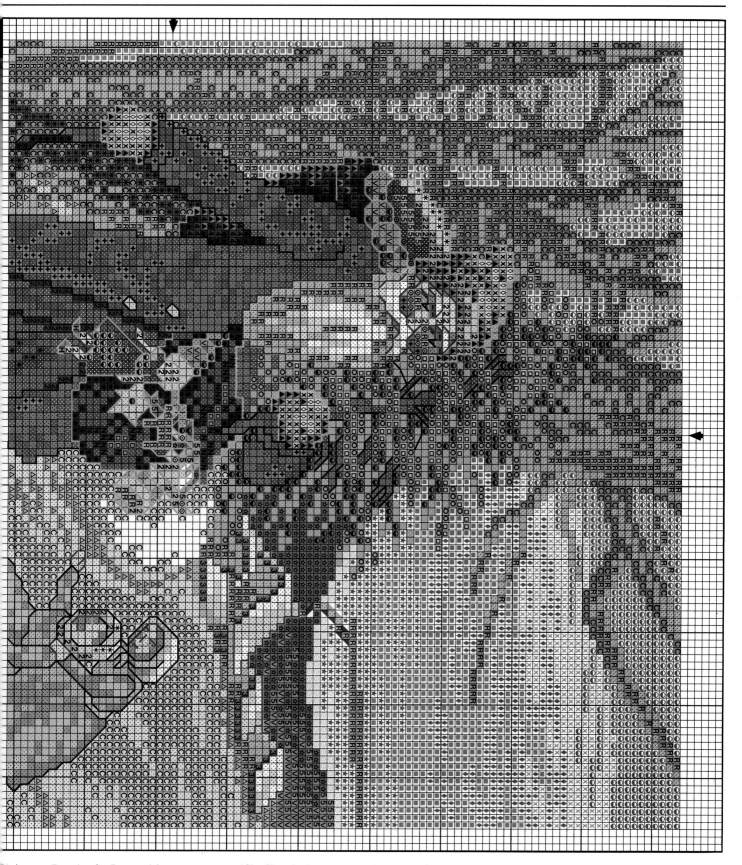

Christmas Traveler in Frame (shown on page 40): The design was stitched over 2 fabric threads on a 17" x 20" piece of Antique White Lugana (25 ct). Three strands of floss were used for Cross Stitch and 1 strand for Half Cross Stitch, Backstitch, and French Knots, unless otherwise noted in the color key. It was custom framed.

Needlework adaptation by Nancy Dockter.

JOY TO THE WORLD

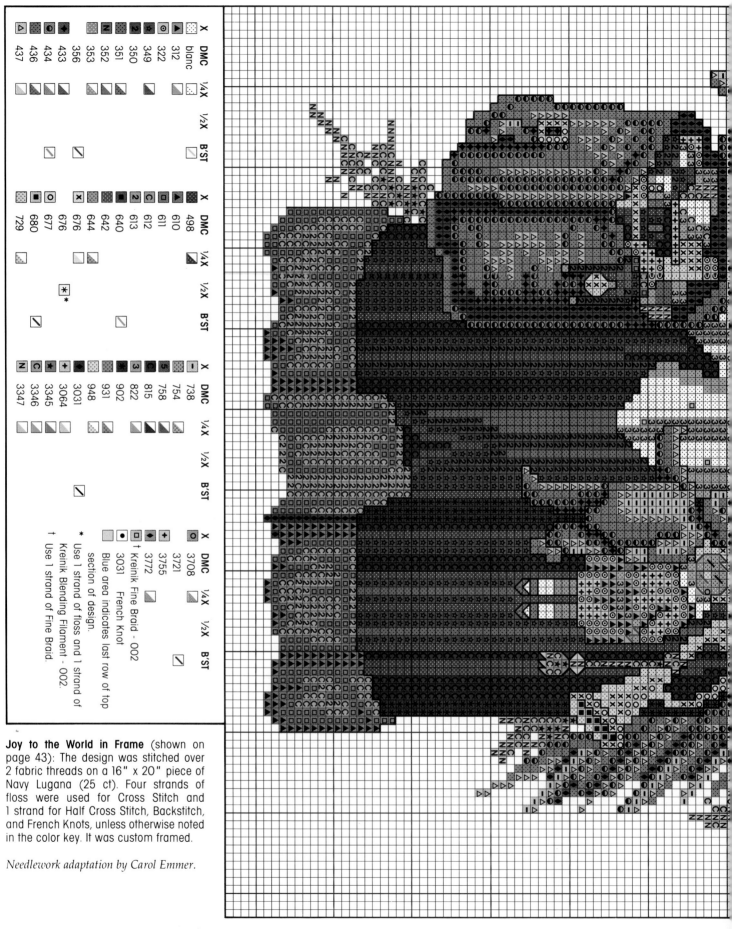

Joy to the World in Frame (shown on page 43): The design was stitched over 2 fabric threads on a 16" x 20" piece of Navy Lugana (25 ct). Four strands of floss were used for Cross Stitch and 1 strand for Half Cross Stitch, Backstitch, and French Knots, unless otherwise noted in the color key. It was custom framed.

Needlework adaptation by Carol Emmer.

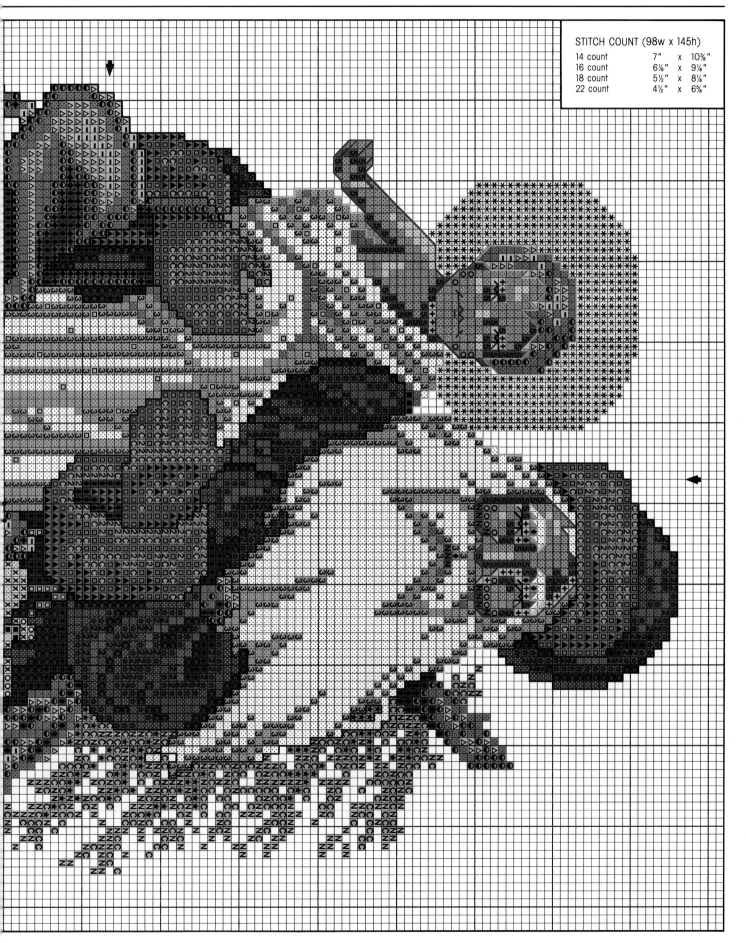

STITCH COUNT (98w x 145h)

14 count	7"	x	10⅜"
16 count	6⅛"	x	9⅛"
18 count	5½"	x	8⅛"
22 count	4½"	x	6⅝"

OLDE WORLD SANTAS

X	DMC	1/4X	1/2X	B'ST
	blanc			
	304			
▲	309			
◉	312			
◆	317			
△	318			
▢	322			
X	335			
■	336			
▦	350			
4	351			
V	353			
✹	356			
▨	413			*
	414			
	415			
	433			
	552			
N	553			
⊙	554			
▦	610			
	611			
	612			*
✳	613			
C	725			
+ †	725			†
	754			
	758			
☆	760			
	762			
▲	780			
	781			
−	783			
	813			
■	814			
	816			*
S	817			*
	822			
✱	895			
3	898			*
★	904			
3	905			
✦	906			
	948			
⊙	986			*
V	3024			
■	3031			
◇	3033			
	3371			
	3770			
▢	3782			
▦	3799			
●	304	French Knot		
◐	762	French Knot		
●	816	French Knot		
◑	3799	French Knot		

* Use 413 for Design #4. Use 612 for Design #5. Use 817 for Design #2. Use 898 for Design #1. Use 986 for Design #3.
† Add 1 strand of Kreinik Blending Filament - 002.

#1 (27w x 100h)

#2 (27w x 100h)

#3 (27w x 100h) **#4 (27w x 100h)** **#5 (31w x 100h)**

Olde World Santa Ornaments (shown on pages 44-45): Each design was stitched on an Ecru Stitch-N-Mark™ bookmark (18 ct). Two strands of floss were used for Cross Stitch and 1 strand for Half Cross Stitch, Backstitch, and French Knots, unless otherwise noted in the color key.

Needlework adaptation by Nancy Dockter.

holiday dressing

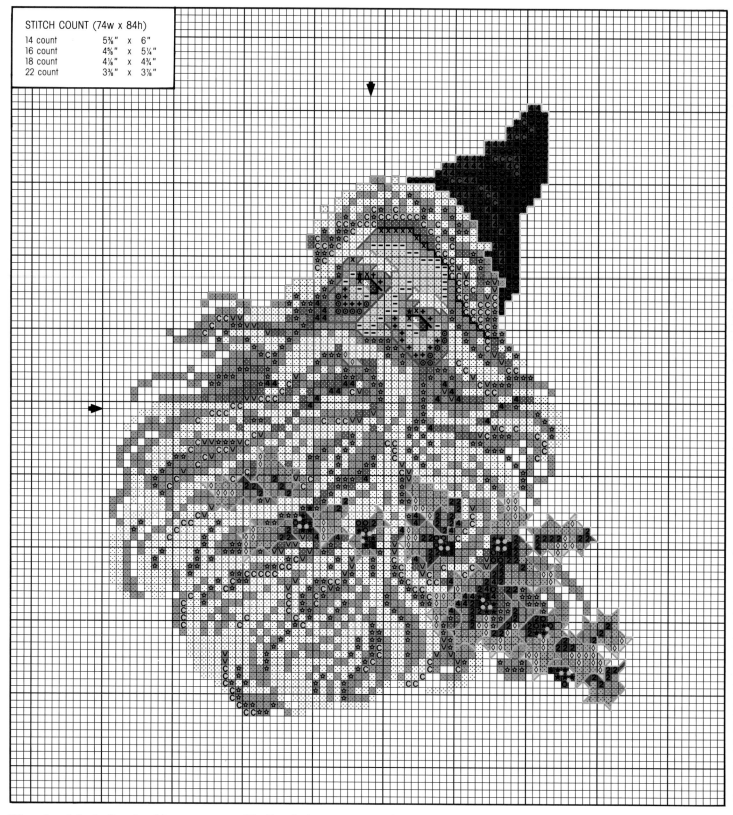

STITCH COUNT (74w x 84h)	
14 count	5⅜" x 6"
16 count	4⅝" x 5¼"
18 count	4⅛" x 4¾"
22 count	3⅜" x 3⅞"

Wispy Beard Santa Sweater (shown on page 49): The design was stitched over an 11" square of 12 mesh waste canvas on a purchased sweater with top of design approximately 1" below bottom of neckband. Four strands of floss were used for Cross Stitch and 1 strand for Backstitch, unless otherwise noted in the color key. (See Working On Waste Canvas, page 92.) Attach beads using 1 strand of DMC 304 floss. (See Attaching Beads, page 95.)

Jingle Bell Santa Sweatshirt (shown on page 47): The design was stitched over a 12" x 9" piece of 12 mesh waste canvas on a purchased sweatshirt with top of design approximately 2" below bottom of neckband. Three strands of floss were used for Cross Stitch and 1 strand for Backstitch and French Knots, unless otherwise noted in the color key. (See Working On Waste Canvas, page 92.)

Refer to photo for placement of desired sizes of jingle bells. Attach bells using 2 strands of DMC 310 floss.

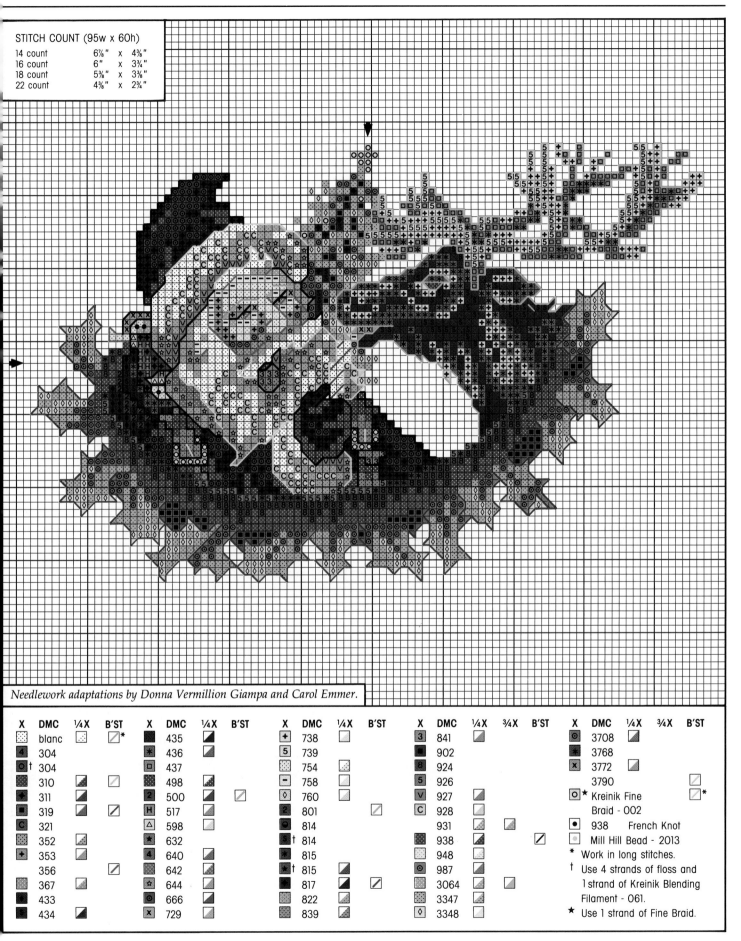

STITCH COUNT (95w x 60h)

14 count	6⅞"	x 4⅜"
16 count	6"	x 3¾"
18 count	5⅜"	x 3⅜"
22 count	4⅜"	x 2¾"

Needlework adaptations by Donna Vermillion Giampa and Carol Emmer.

X	DMC	¼X	B'ST		X	DMC	¼X	B'ST		X	DMC	¼X	B'ST		X	DMC	¼X	¾X	B'ST		X	DMC	¼X	¾X	B'ST
	blanc		*			435				+	738				3	841					⊙	3708			
4	304				*	436				5	739					902					*	3768			
⊙†	304					437					754				8	924					X	3772			
	310					498				−	758				5	926						3790			*
+	311				2	500				◊	760				V	927					⊙★	Kreinik Fine			
	319				H	517				2	801				C	928						Braid - 002			
C	321				△	598				⊙	814					931					●	938 French Knot			
	352				★	632				S†	814					938						Mill Hill Bead - 2013			
+	353				4	640				*	815					948					*	Work in long stitches.			
	356					642				★†	815				⊙	987					†	Use 4 strands of floss and			
	367				☆	644					817					3064						1 strand of Kreinik Blending			
	433				⊙	666					822					3347						Filament - 061.			
	434				X	729					839				◊	3348					★	Use 1 strand of Fine Braid.			

91

holiday dressing

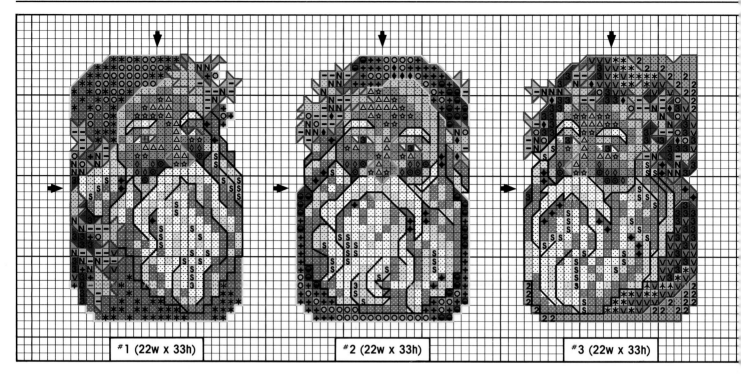

| #1 (22w x 33h) | #2 (22w x 33h) | #3 (22w x 33h) |

Santa Necklace (shown on page 48): Designs #1 and #3 above and Design #2 (chart on page 88; omit background and snow) were each stitched on a 7" square of Ivory Hardanger (22 ct). One strand of floss was used for Cross Stitch and Backstitch.

For necklace, you will need three 7" squares of lightweight cream fabric for backing, 24" necklace, various size charms, 5mm jump rings, three 1½" lengths of ¹⁄₁₆"w ribbon, fabric stiffener, small foam brush, and clear-drying craft glue. See Stiffening Instructions, page 76, to stiffen each design. Fold one length of ribbon in half, matching short edges; refer to photo and glue to wrong side of one stiffened design. Repeat with remaining ribbon lengths and stiffened designs. Using jump rings, refer to photo to attach charms and stiffened designs to necklace.

Needlework adaptation by Nancy Dockter and Donna Vermillion Giampa.

Santa Face Button Covers (shown on page 49): Designs #1, #2, and #3 were each stitched on a 4" square of Ivory Hardanger (22 ct). One strand of floss was used for Cross Stitch and Backstitch.

For each button cover, you will need a 4" square of lightweight cream fabric for backing, ⅝" button cover, fabric stiffener, small foam brush, and clear-drying craft glue. See Stiffening Instructions, page 76, to stiffen each design; glue button cover to back of stiffened design.

Mistletoe Santa Sweater (shown on page 48): Design #4 was stitched over a 10" square of 12 mesh waste canvas on a purchased sweater with top of design approximately 1¾" below bottom of neckband. Three strands of floss were used for Cross Stitch and 1 strand for Backstitch, unless otherwise noted in the color key.

For berries, refer to photo for placement of 4mm pearls and Mill Hill Beads - 40556. Attach berries using nylon thread and a fine needle that will pass through pearl. Bring needle up through design and thread through pearl and bead. Take needle back down through pearl and design, secure thread on back or move to next bead.

Santa Face Candle Ties (shown on page 14): Each design was stitche on a 4" square of Ivory Aida (18 ct). Two strands of floss were used fc Cross Stitch and 1 strand for Backstitch.

For each candle tie, you will need a 4" square of lightweight crear fabric for backing, 34" length of ¹⁄₁₆" dia. gold cord, fabric stiffener small foam brush, and clear-drying craft glue. Follow Stiffenin Instructions (page 76) to stiffen each design. Fold length of gold cord i half and refer to photo to center and glue folded end to back c stiffened design. Tie around decorated candles as desired.

Needlework adaptation by Donna Vermillion Giampa.

WORKING ON WASTE CANVAS

Waste canvas is a special canvas that provides an evenweave grid fc placing stitches on fabric. After the design is worked over the canva: the canvas threads are removed leaving the design on the fabric. Th canvas is available in several mesh sizes.

Cover edges of canvas with masking tape. Cut a piece of lightweigh non-fusible interfacing the same size as canvas to provide a fir stitching base.

Find desired stitching area and mark center of area with a pir Match center of canvas to pin. Use the blue threads in canvas to plac canvas straight on garment; pin canvas to garment. Pin interfacing t wrong side of garment. Baste all layers together as shown in **Fig. 1**.

Using a sharp needle, work design, stitching from large holes t large holes. Trim canvas to within ¾" of design. Dampen canvas unt it becomes limp. Pull out canvas threads one at a time using tweezer (**Fig. 2**). Trim interfacing close to design.

Fig. 1

Fig. 2

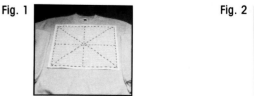

X	DMC	¼X	B'ST		X	DMC	¼X	B'ST		X	DMC	¼X	B'ST		X	DMC	¼X	B'ST
	blanc					754					926					3347		
V*	blanc					760					927					3348		
	312					761					928					3750		
O	321					776					930					3752		
*	322					781	+				935				X	3753		
	451		†			783					937				O	3755		
	452					815					938				2	3756		
-	453				S	822				N	986					3770		
	498					823				-	988					3772		
	504				N	840					3021		†			3773		
	632				C	841					3031					3774		
	640		★			890					3032					3781		
	644					891					3064				V	3790		★
+	725				2	899				2	3345					Kreinik Fine Braid - 002		
	727					902					3346							

* Use 3 strands of floss and 1 strand of Kreinik Blending Filament - 032.

† For Design #4, use 451. For Designs #1, #2, and #3, use 3021.

★ For Designs #1, #2, and #3, use 640. For Design #4, use 3790.

+ Use 3 strands of floss and 1 strand of Kreinik Blending Filament - 002.

○ For Design #1, use 823 for clothes and 902 for berries. For Design #2, use 902. For Design #4, use 938.

‡ Use 1 strand of Fine Braid.

#4 (70w x 73h)

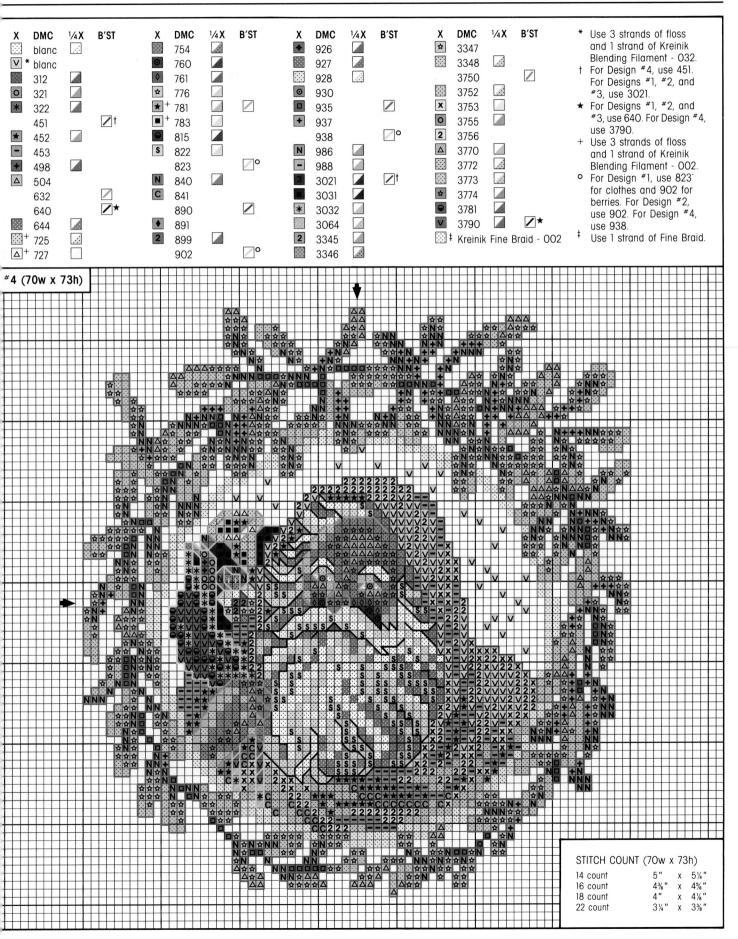

STITCH COUNT (70w x 73h)		
14 count	5"	x 5¼"
16 count	4⅜"	x 4⅝"
18 count	4"	x 4⅛"
22 count	3¼"	x 3⅜"

GENERAL INSTRUCTIONS

WORKING WITH CHARTS

How to Read Charts: Each of the designs is shown in chart form. Each colored square on the chart represents one Cross Stitch or one Half Cross Stitch. Each colored triangle on the chart represents one One-Quarter Stitch or one Three-Quarter Stitch. Black or colored dots represent French Knots or bead placement. The black or colored straight lines on the chart indicate Backstitch. When a French Knot or Backstitch covers a square, the symbol is omitted.

Each chart is accompanied by a color key. This key indicates the color of floss to use for each stitch on the chart. The headings on the color key are for Cross Stitch (**X**), DMC color number (**DMC**), One-Quarter Stitch (**¼X**), Three-Quarter Stitch (**¾X**), Half Cross Stitch (**½X**), and Backstitch (**B'ST**). Color key columns should be read vertically and horizontally to determine type of stitch and floss color.

Where to Start: The horizontal and vertical centers of each charted design are shown by arrows. You may start at any point on the charted design, but be sure the design will be centered on the fabric. Locate the center of fabric by folding in half, top to bottom and again left to right. On the charted design, count the number of squares (stitches) from the center of the chart to where you wish to start. Then from the fabric's center, find your starting point by counting out the same number of fabric threads (stitches). (**Note:** To work over two fabric threads, count out twice the number of fabric threads.)

How To Determine Finished Size: The finished size of your design will depend on the **thread count per inch** of the fabric being used. To determine the finished size of the design on different fabrics, divide the number of squares (stitches) in the width of the charted design by the thread count of the fabric. For example, a charted design with a width of 80 squares worked on 14 count Aida will yield a design 5¾" wide. Repeat for the number of squares (stitches) in the height of the charted design. (**Note:** To work over two fabric threads, divide the number of squares by one-half the thread count.) Then add the amount of background you want plus a generous amount for finishing.

STITCH DIAGRAMS

Note: Bring threaded needle up at 1 and all odd numbers and down at 2 and all even numbers.

Counted Cross Stitch (X): Work one Cross Stitch to correspond to each colored square on the chart. For horizontal rows, work stitches in two journeys (**Fig. 1**). For vertical rows, complete each stitch as shown (**Fig. 2**). When working over two fabric threads, work Cross Stitch as shown in **Fig. 3**. When the chart shows a Backstitch crossing a colored square (**Fig. 4**), a Cross Stitch should be worked first; then the Backstitch (**Fig. 9 or 10**) should be worked on top of the Cross Stitch.

Fig. 1

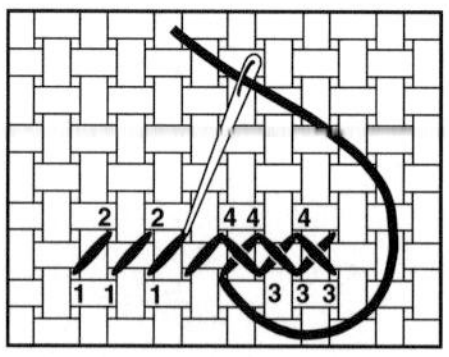

Fig. 2

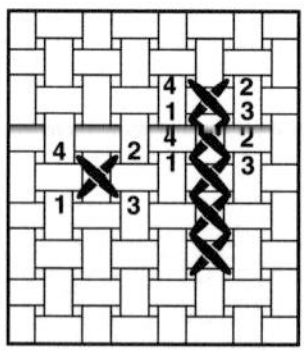

Fig. 3

Fig. 4

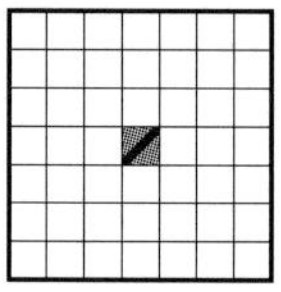

Quarter Stitch (¼X and ¾X): Quarter Stitches are denoted by triangular shapes of color on the chart and on the color key. For One-Quarter Stitch, come up at 1 (**Fig. 5**); then split fabric thread to go down at 2. When stitches 1-4 are worked in the same color, the resulting stitch is called a Three-Quarter Stitch (**¾X**). **Fig. 6** shows the technique for Quarter Stitches when working over two fabric threads.

Fig. 5

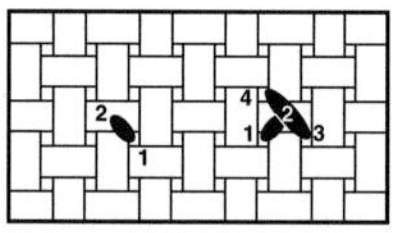

Fig. 6

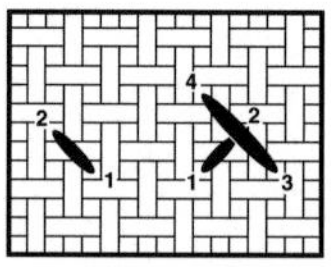

Half Cross Stitch (½X): This stitch is one journey of the Cross Stitch and is worked from lower left to upper right as shown in **Fig. 7**. When working over two fabric threads, work Half Cross Stitch as shown in **Fig. 8**.

Fig. 7

Fig. 8

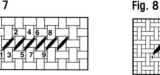

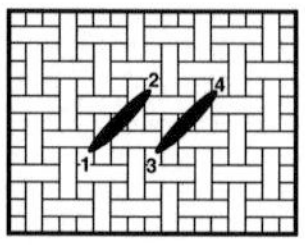

Backstitch (B'ST): For outline detail, Backstitch (shown on chart and on color key by black or colored straight lines) should be worked after the design has been completed (**Fig. 9**). When working over two fabric threads, work Backstitch as shown in **Fig. 10**.

Fig. 9

Fig. 10

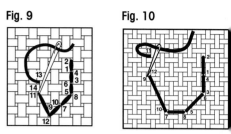

French Knot: Bring needle up at 1. Wrap floss once around needle and insert needle at 2, holding end of floss with non-stitching fingers (**Fig. 11**). Tighten knot; then pull needle through fabric, holding floss until it must be released. For larger knot, use more strands; wrap only once.

Fig. 11

Overcast Stitch: This stitch is used on plastic canvas to cover edges and to join canvas pieces (**Fig. 12**). For even coverage, it may be necessary to go through the same hole more than once, especially at corners.

Fig. 12

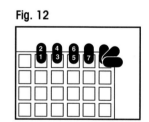

STITCHING TIPS

Working Over Two Fabric Threads: Use the sewing method instead of the stab method when working over two fabric threads. To use the sewing method, keep your stitching hand on the right side of the fabric (instead of stabbing the fabric with the needle and taking your stitching hand to the back of the fabric to pick up the needle). With the sewing method, you take the needle down and up with one stroke instead of two. To add support to stitches, it is important that the first Cross Stitch is placed on the fabric with stitch 1-2 beginning and ending where a vertical fabric thread crosses over a horizontal fabric thread (**Fig. 13**). When the first stitch is in the correct position, the entire design will be placed properly, with vertical fabric threads supporting each stitch.

Fig. 13

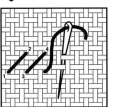

Working With Plastic Canvas: To determine accurate placement of design on canvas, count canvas **threads** (lines) and not **holes** (**Fig. 14**).

Fig. 14

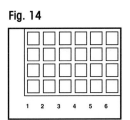

Attaching Beads: Refer to chart for bead placement and sew bead in place using a fine needle that will pass through bead. Bring needle up at 1, run needle through bead then down at 2 making a Half Cross Stitch (**Fig. 15**). Secure floss on back or move to next bead as shown in **Fig. 15**.

Fig. 15

PILLOW FINISHING

Santa and Girl Pillow Finishing (shown on page 12, chart on page 62): For pillow, you will need two 13" squares of fabric for pillow front and backing, 6" dia. circle of craft fleece for padding stitched piece, 2" x 27" bias fabric strip for cording, 27" length of 1/4" dia. purchased cord, 54" length of 1 1/4"w purchased fringe (width includes 1/2" bound edge), and polyester fiberfill.

Centering design, trim stitched piece to a 7" dia. circle.

Center cord on wrong side of bias strip; matching long edges, fold strip over cord. Use a zipper foot to baste along length of strip close to cord; trim seam allowance to 1/2". Matching raw edges, pin cording to right side of stitched piece. Ends of cording should overlap approximately 2"; pin overlapping end out of the way. Starting 2" from beginning end of cording and ending 4" from overlapping end, baste cording to stitched piece. On overlapping end of cording, remove 2 1/2" of basting; fold end of fabric back and trim cord so that it meets beginning end of cord. Fold end of fabric under 1/2"; wrap fabric over beginning end of cording. Finish basting cording to stitched piece; press seam allowance toward stitched piece. Place fleece on wrong side of stitched piece (with fleece between stitched piece and seam allowance).

To attach stitched piece to pillow front, center wrong side of stitched piece on right side of one 13" square of fabric; pin in place. Carefully hand sew stitched piece to pillow front by sewing through all layers as close as possible to cording. Take care not to catch fabric of stitched piece.

Matching raw edges of fabric and bound edge of fringe, pin fringe to right side of pillow front; trim overlapping end to meet beginning end. Baste fringe to pillow front. Matching right sides and leaving an opening for turning, use a 1/2" seam allowance to sew pillow front and backing fabric together. Trim seam allowances diagonally at corners; turn pillow right side out carefully pushing corners outward. Stuff pillow with polyester fiberfill and blind stitch opening closed.

Hooded Santa Pillow Finishing (shown on page 13, chart on page 78): For pillow, you will need a 9 3/8" square of fabric for pillow backing, 6" x 75" strip of fabric for ruffle (pieced as necessary), 2" x 39 1/2" bias fabric strip for cording, 39 1/2" length of 1/4" dia. purchased cord, and polyester fiberfill.

Centering design, trim stitched piece to measure 9 3/8" square.

Center cord on wrong side of bias strip; matching long edges, fold strip over cord. Use a zipper foot to baste along length of strip close to cord; trim seam allowance to 1/2". Matching raw edges, pin cording to right side of stitched piece making a 3/8" clip in seam allowance of cording at corners. Ends of cording should overlap approximately 2"; pin overlapping end out of the way. Starting 2" from beginning end of cording and ending 4" from overlapping end, baste cording to stitched piece. On overlapping end of cording, remove 2 1/2" of basting; fold end of fabric back and trim cord so that it meets beginning end of cord. Fold end of fabric under 1/2"; wrap fabric over beginning end of cording. Finish basting cording to stitched piece.

For ruffle, press short ends of fabric strip 1/2" to wrong side. Matching wrong sides and long edges, fold strip in half; press. Machine baste 1/2" from raw edges, gather fabric strip to fit stitched piece. Matching raw edges, pin ruffle to right side of stitched piece overlapping short ends 1/4". Use a 1/2" seam allowance to sew ruffle to stitched piece.

Matching right sides and leaving an opening for turning, use a 1/2" seam allowance to sew stitched piece and backing fabric together. Trim seam allowances diagonally at corners; turn pillow right side out carefully pushing corners outward. Stuff pillow with polyester fiberfill and blind stitch opening closed.

Instructions tested and photo items made by Lisa Arey, Kandi Ashford, Debbie Bashaw, Marsha Besancon, Karen Brogan, Beth Curry, Natalie DeAngelis, Sharla Dunigan, Marilyn Fendley, Elaine Garrett, Joyce Graves, Muriel Hicks, Diana Hoke, Joyce Holland, Patricia Jones, Arthur Jungnickel, Melanie Long, Susan McDonald, Colleen Moline, Martha Nolan, Ray Ellen Odle, Patricia O'Neil, Sandy Pigue, Sandra Price, Susan Sego, Karen Sisco, Amy Taylor, Mary Tedford, Annette Tracy, Karen Tyler, Jane Walker, Kathy Werkmeister, and Marie Williford.

Continued on page 96.

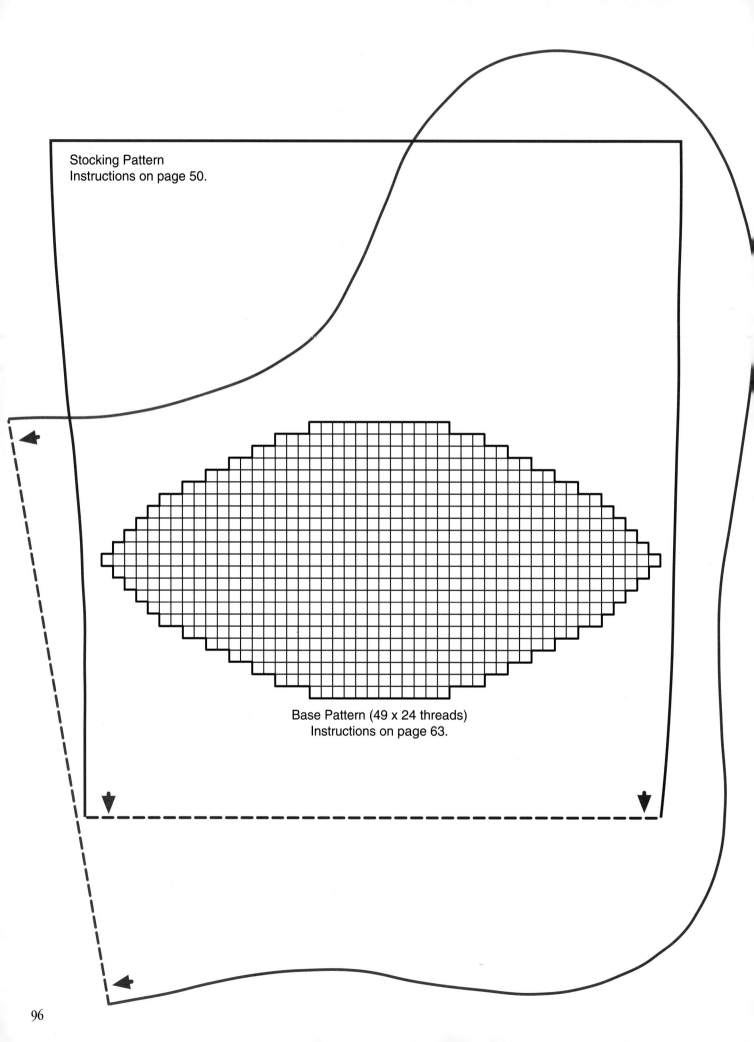

Stocking Pattern
Instructions on page 50.

Base Pattern (49 x 24 threads)
Instructions on page 63.